The Black and White of It

Debby Young

ISBN 979-8-88832-550-6 (paperback)
ISBN 979-8-88832-551-3 (digital)

Christian Faith Publishing
832 Park Avenue
Meadville, PA 16335
www.christianfaithpublishing.com

Printed in the United States of America

First and foremost to my dearest friend, Jesus Christ. Without him, I am nothing. I owe my life to you. You gave yours for me.

Second, to my mother who has always been there for me. You never missed an event—from track and field, swimming, gymnastics, ballet, Girl Scouts, debate clubs, and African dancing events. You made them all, and I thank you, Mom, for always being there for me. With seven kids, I still don't know how you did it, but I'm thankful.

Later as an adult, you were there to support me when I graduated from college, when I was ordained as a pastor and when I started the church. You were there also for my marriages, one divorce, and the burial of a spouse. I love you so much. You're amazing at eighty-nine.

Third, to my one and only child—my daughter Tayona. You're maturing into a beautiful woman and mother. You're the best daughter ever. Thanks for all your caring love and support. I love you.

Fourth, to my grandchildren and godchildren who light up my life with their smiles. I love you all. To my stepchildren, I love you and thank you for allowing me in your lives.

Finally, to my loving husband, John. Thank you for never giving up the chase.

There's no me without you. I'm so glad you're in my life. I love and respect you deeply. You are my king!

FOREWORD

This book has been a long time coming. Many times, I thought of writing it, but the timing wasn't right. I've always wanted to share my life story in its completion in hopes of helping someone else. I'm thankful that the opportunity to pour out my life in black and white is now.

I truly hope that it is taken in and received in the way it's given—in love and forgiveness to all and myself. It is not my intention to embarrass or harm anyone. In my story, I take ownership of the parts I played. It is my prayer that everyone else will eventually do so as well.

God gave me life. I lived it very recklessly at times. There were also those times I wasn't given a choice. I believe everyone should have choices without force. God himself gives us the right to choose.

There were many times in my life when I made major mistakes with free choice. I now can say that I live without regrets. I know now that there is a time and purpose to all things. The Word of God states that God is working it all out for our good. When I chose God as my personal Savior and asked him to receive his Holy Spirit, that's when I truly changed. I now know that not only am I loved, but I also deserve to be loved. That's something I did not believe in for a long time. I'm so grateful to God for keeping me alive long enough to find out that he loves me and always has—just as I am. I thank him for picking up my broken pieces.

Come and join me in my journey in the black and white of it.

CHAPTER 1

Conception

It was in the Summer of 1957. I was born on April 16, 1958. My mom and dad dated about a year before conceiving me. They were not married. In the case where opposites do attract, it would have been befitting for this couple.

My mom was from Washington State far North, and my dad was from Louisiana far South. My mom was and is talkative while my dad was and is fairly quiet. My dad was a drinker and enjoyed bars, and my mom has never had a drink and loved opera and ballet. Opposites!

My mom didn't drink or dance, but her sisters did. She had eight of them and four brothers. Her sisters would go out to the bars on the weekends, and she would go out with them not to be left behind. Back in that day, blacks who dated didn't go to operas and ballets as she would have preferred. She would hang out and get in where she could fit in, as they say.

That's how she met my dad. They had a rocky relationship because of their difference from the start. Pregnancy didn't make it much better. They parted ways before I was born. She was seeing him a few times during my first year, and that was it. That was the start of my life—abandonment.

My dad moved on. He met and moved in with the woman he has been with for almost fifty-six years. My mother was left to raise me on her own, along with her first three children. My siblings' father left my mom with a daughter from another woman, his son, and a sister—my mom's first child. He went to the store and never came back home. That was my mother's first husband.

She was now a mother to four children with no husband, and my dad was the third man to leave her to fend for her own. Amazingly, I never heard one negative word about any one of them from my mom. She just did what she had to do.

My dad moved on and was soon married to the woman he just celebrated his eightieth birthday with. They've been married for fifty-six years and counting. Amazing! Out of that union came four sisters and brothers I knew of and two others who I just found out about over the last past ten years.

My mother was left to struggle with four children—a daughter from her first husband who left, my brother, my biological older sister, and myself—when he walked out to go to the store and never came back and was never seen by my mother again. My brother and sister, his biological kids, found him much later in a nursing home; and he, Joseph, their father, has since passed away. I'll call Joseph Smith number one.

My mom married four times. Joe was her first husband. I don't remember Joe at all. I was just an infant, but I did take his last name Debby Smith because in those days, you take the husband's name.

CHAPTER 2

All Right with White

When I was two years old, my mother remarried a very tall, intelligent white man. I don't remember the wedding. I was too small, but my memories of having a father were all with him.

As it went, my mother met my stepfather through his sister who was a very good friend to her. They dated for about a year and got married. At that time, mixed marriages were looked down upon by both races, but they both received their families' blessings and were married in Goodwill Baptist Church Seattle, Washington. My mother, by her pictures, was a beautiful bride. My stepdad Bob Grimm (at that time) stood tall in a black suit, looking pretty spiffy himself.

At the time of their marriage, we lived briefly in the Holly Park projects. After marrying, we moved to a large red house on Plum Street near Beacon Hill. I started kindergarten at Van Asselt Elementary School. I attended there for the first half of the year until we moved to Plum. I finished elementary school at John Muir.

Elementary school was great for me. Back in those days, there were no cell phones or video games. We just played games like kickball, tether ball, dodge ball, tag, hopscotch, and jacks. We had three recesses back then. School was lots of fun for me.

For the most part, I was a bright kid and did well academically. My behavior in class could have been better, but I completed it with flying colors. In the '60s, the grades went from K through sixth grade.

My stepfather's side of the family was all white, and my mother's family was all black, but I never was treated any differently by any of them. I knew no difference. On the weekends, we'd all go to my aunt Zetta's house. All the kids would be downstairs. She was an elementary school teacher, so we were always surrounded by books and desks. Playing school was my favorite game.

Upstairs, all the adults—oftentimes my aunts on my mother's side and my aunts and uncles on my father's side—would all be playing their favorite game scrabble and talking about current events and world news. We had holidays together, especially Christmas, and we were all one big happy family. I was loved by all and corrected as well by all. Life as a young child was great.

My step father's mother was a seamstress, so she sewed many of our clothes. My cousins of all colors and I would often have matching clothes. The only difference I ever really noticed as a child was the hair. Theirs was straight, and mine was short and curly.

We all did everything together. My grandma Marge would sew huge fluffy sleeping bags for the entire clan, and our vacations would be on the Pacific Ocean Oregon Coast out in the open next to a campfire. Very seldom do I remember a tent. We were free to roam the ocean shores and the hills. We were all always together. White, black, and mixed, that was us.

When we weren't on the beach, we were climbing Mount Rainier and jumping and swimming in the icy cold mountain waters. Life was great. The outdoor was a big playground for my brother, sisters, and cousins. Everything was all right with black and white.

CHAPTER 3

I remember leaving the house on Plum and moving to a red house, and it was a lot bigger in the red house. I left Van Asselt grade K and transferred to John Muir grade K. It didn't take me long to adjust to my new school. I loved the teacher. I was actually way ahead from being at Van Asselt and playing school with older siblings and cousins. Remember that my aunt, Aunt Zetta, was an elementary teacher. That helped immensely.

School was good; life was good. The red house had a big yard with lots of trees, and that's where I played. My best friends were a grade above me, and they were twins—Heckel and Jeckel, named after cartoon birds.

They got teased, but they were my friends, and most of my time after school was with them. At the time, I was the youngest of four, but not for long. My stepfather and mother found the red house to be much too drafty and hard to heat, so it was then that we moved about five blocks to the white house on the hill.

CHAPTER 4

The White House

The white house was quite adventurous. I say that because we had a lot of property full of cherry trees, plum trees, grapes, and blackberries in the fall! My stepfather was a builder and had built us a two-story treehouse with a patio roof. There were two ways to access it and three ways to exit. You could climb up the initial tree on ladder steps that were built into the tree, or you could climb up the tree opposite the treehouse and walk across on a thick rope plank on the bottom and a thin rope to hold onto on top. To exit, you could do the same, the steps or plank, but he also added a pulley where you could zip-line down. There was none in the neighborhood like ours.

The claw-foot bathtub was taken out and became our summer swimming pool. The previous bathtub had now been replaced with unfinished bricks—another unfinished project by my dad. (This was a habit that irritated my mother continually—unfinished projects.)

One year, we went on a family vacation through the Redwood forest on the way to one of our many trips to the ocean. As a kid, seeing the enormity of those huge beautiful trees was breathtaking. Driving through the base was one I was so delighted about. We traveled a lot and got stickers from many of our visits to well-known landmarks.

CHAPTER 5

Primary School

John Muir was a very multicultural school. My friends consisted of Hanna, a first-generation Hawaiian American; Gloria, a native Indian; Cindy was white, Bella was from Greece; and Denise, a black or should I say brown.

Every morning, my mother would comb my hair and send me out the door to a waiting friend. I could say that I was very popular at school. I was always very athletic and smart too. I was quick at most everything, which caused a lot of problems in class. I would finish before others, get bored, and get in trouble talking all the time. My wittiness kept me in trouble in a lot of ways. I was often challenging the teachers and students. It was too bad they didn't have debate classes in elementary school. Unfortunately, my wits got me sent to the principal's office quite frequently, which didn't sit too well with my mother who was usually the disciplinarian along with the help from a willow tree.

Life, for the most part, was good. Like I said previously, we went to school, did our chores, and played until sundown then started over again. Being outdoors was my favorite pastime. It was in the white house where my stepfather adopted us, and we became Grimms legally after our stepfather Bob Grimm.

This was in the mid-'60s. Motown was growing rapidly. Music and dancing were one of my joys. On a trip to Disneyland at ten years old, my mother and dad thought my sister and I were lost.

The entire family looked for us for hours only to find my baby sister, who was five at the time, and myself on the dance floor doing the monkey dance and the jerk. We were surrounded by a crowd who'd thrown dollars and change galore for our outstanding dancing skills. My mother was livid but relieved, needless to say.

In fourth and fifth grades, the civil rights movement was quite actively gaining way. I didn't have a clue of the extent and was black-and-white. I thought, *How can I choose sides when I have so much love from both sides?* You see, I had both white and black grandmothers, white and black aunts and uncles, and white and black cousins and friends. I didn't see any effects at home right then, but it soon would infiltrate our family in the worst way. I was nine or ten.

The white house was located in the south end of Seattle on top of a big hill, and on the back side were a few homes and apartments. On the front side, there was a business and a small store called Mr. Pinuckles after the store owner. Mr. Pinuckles sold candies, gums, and snacks. There were a few groceries in the store, but we, kids, bought treats. At that time, the price was five pieces for a penny. Imagine that. A penny really did buy a lot back then.

Across the street from Mr. Pinuckles was a business I never knew the name of, but it had the coldest water fountain in town, and we'd run in and drink so we would be refreshed. Even though the civil rights movement became very active in the late '60s, I didn't have a clue of its extent and the effect it would have on our interracial family.

CHAPTER 6

The workers knew we shouldn't be there. Never once did they turn us away. The silver water fountains are the ones I look for even to this day.

Down the street from Mr. Pinuckles was Safeway Store where my mother would sometimes send us kids for flour or sugar and extra things needed. It's also where, for the first time, I decided to steal some candy and got caught. I couldn't imagine the fear I had when I thought they were going to call my mom. They didn't, but they threatened me and told me not to come back to the store. What a time! I would make excuses after that when my mom would try to send me back there like, "Why I couldn't go to Safeway?"

On a trip back from Safeway with my brother (he went in the store), I can remember experiencing my first sight of abuse. A woman ran out of her house looking like she had been fighting. She ran up to me and my brother and asked us to call the police, and she gave us a dollar a piece and a change for the phone booth, and we did. I don't know what happened, but it was scary.

The house, two doors up on the backside, used to have a sign that says, "Beware of Kangaroo." And we, kids, used to be so scared, thinking there was a large kangaroo in that house, not knowing it was placed there jokingly.

The walk to the school arena from the white house was through an alley about two blocks. There were lots of apple trees and fruit trees. We were chased out of yards constantly. Besides our penny candy, I really don't remember having a lot of store-bought snacks. We basically lived off fruits in all seasons. My mom loved to bake, and we'd pick the fruit or berries for the pies. I can remember picking bowls of blackberries, cherries, and plums; the fruit was plentiful and fresh from the trees or bushes.

Throughout the week we went to school, we would do our chores and homework. We would play outside till dinner, bath, and go to bed. Now on the weekends, I'd be the first one up on Saturday. That's when I was allowed to watch Saturday morning cartoons such as *Tom and Jerry*, the *Road Runner Show*, *Mickey Mouse*, and Tweety Bird. Those were the days. During the week, we would watch very little TV. In the morning, while Mom was combing my hair, I was allowed to watch *J. P. Patches Show*. He was a live clown, somewhat equal to a character on *Sesame Street*. I was also allowed to watch *Captain Kangaroo*. *J. P. Patches Show* allowed different groups to be taped live. Once, my sister and her Girl Scout troop were on TV. That was a big deal.

One weekend, when my cousins were over, we thought our dog, Patches, a speckled dog, could fly after watching the movie *Dumbo*. *It was* about the flying elephant. We threw Patches from the roof over the garage. Well, he couldn't thank God. He didn't die and just had minor injuries.

The Beatles were really popular back then, and I, being a lover of music, knew every song by them, and so did my sisters. I can remember my oldest sisters and a cousin got tickets to go see the Beatles My oldest sister, Lil, got in trouble and wasn't allowed to go. She unsuccessfully—for a whole week—tried to change my mother's mind. I think she cried for a whole day. That was my mom then and still is today. Her yes means yes, and no is no. She was and is always consistent with that.

I loved music, and at every opportunity to enter a talent show, I was there. Mimicking the Supremes's "Stop! In the Name of Love" or Jimmy Mack's "Going to the Chapel of Love," and even the Hawaiian Hukilau dance. It didn't matter. I loved all kinds of music and dance. Thank goodness that John Muir gave us lots of opportunities to express that love.

My second favorite thing next to music was sports. You name it, I'd play it—baseball, kickball, dodgeball, football, tetherball. I actually got a tetherball for one Christmas. You couldn't keep me away from the playground where the poles were. Track and field was my ultimate favorite. There was no girl in the school who could beat me in the fifty-yard dash. I was what they called a tomboy.

We were not allowed to wear pants back then, so some creativity is called for to climb the top of the monkey bars and swing upside. Thank God for tights. We had three recesses in school, and I looked forward to them all. We played hard. They also had a presidential achievement award for those who were quite athletics. That would be me doing one hundred sit-sups, push-ups, jump ropes, and squats. I made it each year I attended elementary.

My third-grade teacher was a beautiful woman, and she's one of the few teachers I can remember. Her name was Ms. Jefferies. I'll never forget when she became pregnant and had to leave school in the middle of the year. I was devasted.

I don't remember much about my fourth-grade teacher, but my fifth-grade teacher wasn't the nicest. I can remember an incident where Robert Gadberry (my fifth-grade boyfriend if you can have one, really) was looking at a magazine he'd brought to class, and she came up behind me and pulled the chair out from under me. It hurt so bad (it still does sometimes if I sit too long). I didn't know then, but I know how that shouldn't have happened because she cracked my coccyx bone. I didn't tell my mother until I became an adult and had problems with it. I was afraid at that time that I'd get in trouble with her for talking in class.

Robert Gadberry was my first crush. He was a very cute, green-eyed blond-haired young boy. We seemed to stay in trouble in that class. During summers when we were in town and not vacationing, we would spend our days at Mount Baker Beach on Lake Washington. It was at that beach where I'd occasionally see my biological father with his children.

My heart seemed to ache to watch them seemingly having such a wonderful time together. It didn't stop my love for the water though. We had a small raft with two diving boards where we'd play rock paper scissors, push and run, and jump and dive from sunup to sunset. The routine was eating breakfast, doing chores, packing lunch, going to the beach, and coming home for dinner at around seven every day during all summer.

It was in the fifth grade that I experienced my second death and a tragedy. We were all on the raft in the beach, on the part where the lifeguards were attending, and I had seen Robert in the swim-at-your-own-risk area on an inner tube, which is what we used to use to float on back then. I never thought it was a big deal at the time. We all kept playing, jumping, and swimming. I remember seeing him way out past the raft and out of the area of the lifeguarded beach. I saw him and a small boy floating on inner tubes. My friend and I waved and kept swimming, and about fifteen minutes later, we looked and found there were only tubes. Both boys had gone down. The lifeguards were alerted, and the beach was cleared. It was horrible. As we sat watching the divers coming up again and again unsuccessfully, our eyes were wet with tears, but my heart was broken. I knew I wouldn't see my boyfriend Robert Gadberry again alive.

They both floated up to shore three days later and were funeralized. The entire community was in shock. The young boy was only seven, and Robert was nine and a half. It was said that the young boy fell off the tube, and Robert went in to save him. They both drowned.

Robert had always been a rule breaker. He broke his last one that day. It took me a while to get over that, as well as the community. In those days, it really was a community. Everyone knew just about everyone. Neighbors were really neighbors. We knew one another by family names—the Jimmersons, Kellys, Standafords, Lopezes Cheatums, Browns, Beemans, Rogers, and Levizos. As you walked down the street, everyone knew you, and you knew everyone.

As a kid, if you'd done something wrong, everyone knew long before you got home, and you got reminded of what was to come along the way by your adult neighbors. It was good because everyone looked out for one another and knew one another by name.

I talked too much in school back then, and everyone knew it and would let me know all the way home. How they knew I'd been to the principal's office is beyond, me but they did. And the willow tree knew. That's where I'd stop to get switches from on the way in.

We spent Christmas Eves at my aunt Zetta's. I remember being very young when she had a new home built on the side of her old one. It was a large home and held all of us comfortably. Upstairs in front of a picture window in the living room would always be a beautiful silver artificial tree, but downstairs in the basement would be the live pine tree that touched the ceiling and came out about four feet.

My eyes would dance at the lighting, the ornaments, and the smell of cranberries, popcorn, and pine I can still remember. And the presents were so many. She went out of her way to make the holidays so special for us, kids. She had no children of her own besides us and the fourth graders she taught at Georgetown Elementary.

I never thought of asking her why she didn't have children. I just gladly received the love she showered on me. She'd always pay my older sister to wash and braid my hair for the holidays, and she'd pay me to scratch and brush hers, which I did gladly and would have done for free.

I was a late bed wetter (almost ten). I remember her getting up in the middle of the night to get me to the bathroom so I wouldn't have an accident. She was an excellent cook, and when I spent the weekends with her, she'd allow me to pick the potatoes and other vegetables from the garden with her and help her with the cooking. She made the best baked potatoes in the world. When I was with her, she made sure I read a lot.

Her house was about thirty minutes out of town, and she'd always have me read out loud sometimes. She had a Chevrolet car made out of real steel. I remember one time we were all riding in the car, and I was reading. I was young and was asked how to spell *shirt*, and I left out the *R*. They laughed, and I didn't understand it then, but they got a kick. Along the way, we'd play the alphabet game. That's where you have to find words that start with each letter of the alphabet (except for *X* which we'd allow by pass). We did this on road trips, and I still do it with my daughter and grandkids today. Reading was and still is my favorite subject. I love words.

CHAPTER 7

Aunt Zetta

My aunt Zetta was white. She was such a great person. God always puts people in my life who truly loved me and cared for me and made my life special, and I felt like I was always special to my aunt Zetta. She would take us to a Catholic church with her relatives and cover our heads with scarves as there were never any other blacks, and they stared. But it never mattered to her. She'd also take us up to the ice creamery where we could sit on counter stools and eat the ice cream of our choice.

In Riverton Heights and around town, everyone knew her and loved her, and they treated us well because of her. Once again, we would get stared at being with this middle-aged white woman with three or four black children. She never seemed to mind. I never once remembered her discussing race. Even though she taught at an all-white grade school, to my knowledge, there was never a negative word mentioned about us or her schoolkids.

She would bring the old textbooks home, and this enabled us to play school because we had several copies of the same books.

Grandma Bankert, Aunt Zetta's mom, lived with her, and we shared birthdays because she was born one day earlier than mine.

CHAPTER 8

The Movement

In the mid-'60s, the civil rights movement was actively in place. I was in the fifth grade when it really affected me, and I begin to look at the black and white of it. There were riots going on. Black power became the latest and greatest slogan. I can remember holding black power signs in the streets with my older sisters. It was during this time that my oldest sister hooked up with a pretty high-ranked Black Panther to my mom and dad's displeasure. It was the first time I felt I had to pick sides.

It was a very hard time for me as a child. It seemed impossible to do anything when my family was mixed, as well as all of my friends. I can remember getting really sick at school one day and my father having to come to get me. Several of my classmates had no idea I had a white father. I was so embarrassed but yet so grateful he had come and rescued me. He had swooped me up out of the classroom and carried me in his arms out of the school and into the car.

In my heart of hearts, he felt like my knight in shining armor— my daddy—like any little girl would feel. But the shame I felt of him being white took away the moment. Now everyone knew. *It is so unfair*, I thought. I just didn't or couldn't understand why the color you are made so much difference. I was about to find out.

When I got back to school, the kids had lots of questions for me. Two days later, I just had a bad cold. I answered in the only way, "I knew how. He married my mother and adopted us." That was the truth, and that's all I knew. At that time, in fifth grade, one of my best friends was Cindy, and she was white and had an aunt her same age. My cousin Rose, when she came over on the weekends, got where she always wanted to fight her. It was nothing she'd do. I believe it was just her color. The area she lived in was predominantly black, and I think she felt it was the thing to do. I used to stop her and tell her she was my friend and that it doesn't matter what color she is.

Does that give you a right to hate her? I didn't get it.

During the movement, several of my relatives (the white ones) were unable to drive through certain areas of the town. They could not shop in certain stores. They were actually warned. One was my aunt Zetta. She was warned not to come out after dark. I cried. I still didn't understand.

Aunt Zetta was my favorite aunt, and she was a wonderful teacher. She was in her sixties, and I thought it was very unfair for her to be treated that way. She hadn't a prejudice bone in her. She was the one who showed me how to garden. I had my own garden at her house. She made sure my sisters and I had ballet, swimming, and gymnastics. Every season, she would take us shopping at Sears to buy seasonal clothing and Easter dresses, and Christmases were spent at her house. She took us to plays and dramas, and we'd have weekend picnics at the zoo regularly with great picnic lunches.

My aunt Zetta never had any kids. She basically made it her business to financially help my parents by giving us the things they couldn't afford to give us. She took care of her elderly mother who we all addressed as Grandma Bankert until she died. Her birthday and mine were a day apart, so we always celebrate together. Aunt Zetta would make us separate homemade cakes.

I loved Grandma Bankert just the same. Her viewing was the first time I witnessed a deceased person. My mom wouldn't allow us to go to the funeral, but I cried for a long time. I can still remember her beautiful face and her hands crossed in the casket.

Why did my aunt Zetta, my lovely aunt, have to be attacked because of her color? I saw fear in her eyes one day as she told my mom about almost being attacked by someone in the central district.

I went to bed scared and worried for my aunt and many of the whites in my family. I don't think my mother even knew I had overheard her dilemma. We were never allowed to be present when adults were talking.

CHAPTER 9

The House on the Lake

At ten years old, my mother, father, sisters, and brothers all build a house from the ground up. I remember carrying wood and handing nails. I was so excited at that time. I thought we were building it for ourselves, but I came to find out later that we build it to sell to have money for a down payment for the big house over the lake one block north of the floating bridge. The house we built on Beacon Hill is still standing.

My stepfather was always having us do projects. He once had us all make shoes. We actually were making shoes. As kids, it was fun because we did everything as a family. We'd cut the leather and place it on the shoe for men, and my father and mother would place a cast in it to form a shoe. We'd come back days later and stick and glue. We really made shoes.

Once we moved into the house over the lake, my father began his projects on the house once again (many of which he did not finish). It was huge. It had three levels. It has a finished basement with a kitchen, upstairs with a full dining room, a big living room, and a huge picture window that looked right over Lake Washington and the floating bridge. My mom and stepdad's room was on the same level. Four more bedrooms were upstairs. My two older sisters shared a room, and my two youngest sisters shared a room. My brother had a room, and I had a beautiful room with windows around, one of which had a sitting place, and huge closets. It was a nice change. My brother and I had shared rooms at the previous house. We moved the summer before I entered the sixth grade.

Fortunately, I got to remain at the same school. It was about a two-mile walk, but back then, that was nothing for us. We walked everywhere practically. It consisted of me walking most of the way right along the lake and through a beautiful park that flowered year-round and had tennis courts. My mother played tennis and had shown us the game on the same courts years earlier.

I really loved the house. It was there that I met my best friend Shauna Rogers. We always went to the same school. I knew of her, but we now live only blocks apart because, as they would say these days, we were BFFs. We did everything together. We walked to school together and back. Her father was an attorney, and her mother was a registered nurse. They were so nice to me and always treated me like I was family. I spent almost every day after school at the Rogers. Her dad was also a coach for the little league football at the Rainier Community Center. (It's a recreational center that had all kinds of activities going on year-round for free. Imagine that.)

I can remember many days walking after school to the playfield (that's where the boys were too) and Mr. Rogers riding us back home in the evenings. It was past the school, so it had to be at least three miles. We walked and talked and shared our innermost secrets—almost. There was one thing I did not share with her. I wish I had but I was fearful, and that was about the next-door neighbor Mr. Wallace.

Like I mentioned before, I was an outdoor kid; and if I wasn't going to Shauna's, I was going up the hill to play or going to the store. One day, I was coming down the stairs. Mr. Wallace's garage was right next to ours, and he was standing inside his garage. He called me, and him being an adult and me being a child, I answered. He beckoned me in from where he was and closed the door. What happened next changed my whole world and my innocence.

He fondled me in my vagina. I had no breasts at that time, or he would have and eventually did as I developed. He gave me some change, warned me not to tell anyone, and sent me on my way. I'd never felt so dirty. I didn't know what to do. I just kept it inside. That's why I say it took my innocence.

Keeping secrets is abnormal for a child, and a dirty secret is even double worse.

I tried to continue to live a normal life, but every time he did it, I'd start back over from climbing out of the pit. It was our dirty little secret, and it went on for almost four years.

I still went to school, stayed involved with sports, became very good at track and field, and kept busy. My friendship with Shauna was a very positive one. I met others who I went to school with and lived up the hill. I joined the Girl Scouts. Mom signed me and my brother up for interchange families when I was ten and my brother was eleven. That meant that white families would come and stay with black families, and black families would go stay with white families for a week or so. This was during the '60s, and the civil rights movement was in full force.

Integration was the popular word. I didn't really understand the gist of it. I was just a kid, and my family was already integrated. That was my thought. Nevertheless, my mom did agree for me and my brother to become interchanged kids during the summer of 1968.

Now my mother's parents rarely left their hometown to stay in Seattle. When they did, it was usually with my aunt Joyce. I remember them staying the night with us and us being happy to have them there visiting. I remember my grandfather. He was tall and strong and had such beautiful white teeth. He was about six feet and two inches, and my grandmother was short at about five feet, but somehow, they complimented each other well. They met after both having been married before. Each had one child. My grandfather had a son, Van Craven, and my grandmother had one daughter, Leola Mae. My grandfather was from Texas, and my grandmother was from Washington state.

Back to the story. My grandfather wasn't feeling well. That's why he came to Seattle. He had come to go to the doctor. There is no hospital in Roslyn.

I remember him going, and the next thing I remember is that, after maybe two or three days, my grandfather died. My mom was devasted. I'd never really seen her sad. My brother and I did not attend the funeral because we were scheduled to go to the Lang family for a week for our interchanged family. My mother and stepfather insisted we stick to what was planned.

CHAPTER 10

The Langs

The Langs were very kind to me and my brother. They lived in Sequim, Washington. They stayed on a large piece of property and had their own small lake with a dock, boat, and canoe. The lake was self-stocked with rainbow trout. The house was huge, and connected to it was another small house where their grandpa and grandma lived. Their family consisted of Mr. Lang, Mrs. Lang, Gary, and Ruth. Gary was a year younger than my brother, and Ruth was a year younger than me.

It turned out to be a wonderful week of fun. It was there that I learned to canoe and row a boat. I could swim as much as I liked. Mrs. Lang was an excellent cook and kept us well-fed. Mrs. Lang always had things planned for us to do, so we stayed busy. Grandpa and Grandma were loving and kind. That summer was the first of the many that we spent at the Langs because they invited us back without the inconvenience of the interchanged program.

Mrs. Lang was a Girl Scout leader, so every summer, we'd go on camping adventures with her Girl Scout troop. One summer, we were in the cabins in the mountains and on lakes boating and swimming. We spent nights around the campfire, singing song after song. I learned from the Girl Scouts how to raise and take down the flag and fold it. We hiked and cooked over the campfire (which I was familiar with because my family camps out yearly). I learned many things during the four years I spent with the Langs.

I can remember one time when the family was barbecuing, and they all ate their steaks rare, and I just knew I couldn't eat it that way. I was scared to tell them because I did not want to offend them. But when they placed my steak in front of me, I almost was in tears. I remember how they laughed not at me but gently consoled me and told me they'd be more than happy to cook it however I wanted it.

They used to have a shoot to throw your laundry in that went from the top floor directly into the laundry room. I thought that was so cool, but I used to worry about just how dirty my clothes were for some reason. Mrs. Lang never complained. She went about taking care of all of us—her husband, us kids, and her parents—with no effort. I really admired her.

Grandad, Mr. Lang, Gary, and my brother Joey would all be watching TV and reading newspapers, and Grandma and Mrs. Lang were scurrying around the house. We, girls, were always talking. Ruth was slightly spoiled, so often, I looked forward to getting to camp with the other girls. I do remember Mrs. Lang reminding me that after all was said and done, I would be returning back to her and Ruth's house once we leave the camp to be kind to her. She was right. I'd been ignoring her, and she was correcting me with love. She seemed okay once we got home, but she didn't invite me back the next summer. I think I hurt her feelings. The last time I saw them was when I was fourteen. I called years later, but I've never seen them again. They played a big part in my life, and I was so grateful for the experience.

CHAPTER 11

When I was eleven, I was continuously being sexually abused by my neighbor weekly. I had actually become used to it, never knowing what day or what time, but I knew he'd be lurking out of that garage door. Unfortunately, there was only one way to get up to the basement entrance or the living room front door, and that was to go up the stairs directly next to the garages.

In my childlike mind, I used to try and come up with ideas on how to get to the entrance in different ways. It never worked. I tried coming home at different times, but he was still lurking there and would grab me in the garage to fulfill his own sick sexual needs without thinking about how I felt. I'd say no and that I didn't want his money. I'd try to run and get away, but he'd still be there.

The way the stairs were situated, no one in either house could see you come up until you reach the top of the first set of stairs. I cried about it many nights, but I never told anyone. I continued trying to live the life of a normal child.

CHAPTER 12

Like I said, I was in Girl Scouts. I learned many things like camping, hiking, sewing, and tying knots. Honor and respect were also taught. I can remember one time I was on my way to a Girl Scout meeting that was going to be at a large park. I had an hour or so before needing to arrive, so I went up the hill to play with some friends on my bike.

We lived on several steep hills. That day, I decided to show off to some little boys who were also riding their bikes downhill. I started down the hill, and about halfway down, I decided to throw my hands up in the air. I shouted to get everyone's attention. "Look at me, no hands!" The next thing I knew, I was flying forward. I hit my chin hard, and there was blood everywhere. I managed to make it home, but I had to go to the hospital and get six stitches.

My mother, being who she is, still marched me to that Girl Scout meeting with the largest bandage on my chin I'd ever seen. What a sight I was. I joined in with the rest of the girls as if nothing happened. I still got a lot of attention, though, by being asked what happened.

From the location of the house on the lake, you could go down the hill one block, and you would literally be right on the lakefront. That's where the Levisos lived. Both their parents were doctors. They had a boat and dock and a beautiful house. Unfortunately, the dad committed suicide, which I didn't understand as a kid because I just knew they had everything. I now know that money can't buy everything. At that time, it was very sad. They were my friends.

CHAPTER 13

Shauna's family, like I said, were actually pretty well-off. The first time I entered their kitchen, I saw so much food I had never seen in my life—noodles and snacks and all kinds of fruits and sweets. They invited me to eat, like I said, just about every night, and I was glad to stay. At my house, we never went hungry, but we definitely did not have snacks and a large abundance of food. I do remember eating a lot of potatoes. Our fruit had always come from the trees and vines in our yard. Our snack on Fridays sometimes would be popcorn. Occasionally, my mother would bake oatmeal or chocolate chip cookies.

The Rogers' house, though, was always full of everything. They also had the cutest black mutt named Soul. Every time I'd knock, he'd bounce down the stairs awaiting me. He was definitely part of the family. Shauna's family also had a large Winnebago. During the summer, they'd often be gone for weeks to Montana to visit her grandparents and other family members.

Shauna had two sisters and one brother, and they also loved and treated me like family. During Christmas, they would all get watches from their grandparents and so many gifts. At our house, the gifts were minimum, but we always got something, and then we also had Christmas at aunt Zetta's house too.

I can remember being about eleven and a half or twelve, and Shauna liked this particular boy who lived near us. His family was well-off. During one of their phone calls one day, he had a call waiting way back then. She found out he was saying, "Wait a minute," and had another girl on the phone all the time. I remember she was so mad about it.

Shauna and I, as I stated, shared everything. I can remember how jealous I was. We were both waiting to be "grown-ups" (having our menses), and she started first. Unusually though, she only had two periods, and then it stopped for a year. In actuality, I started at twelve, and she started back months after me. That was so important to us.

As I think back now, the reason I was running track is that Mr. Rogers and his family and my family were all very supportive. His name for me was Speedy Butt. I adored it. It was truly like having two sets of parents.

At eleven, my brother and I were allowed to ride the bus to friends and families in the central area. They'd have something called an all-day pass for one dollar, and you could ride the bus on the weekend wherever you wanted to go. Our bus stop happened to be at the end of the line. This meant that the bus would park for about ten to fifteen minutes and start back on the same route he'd come.

The number of the bus was the twenty-seventh, and it was in Yesler. Yesler Street in those days was very active. We're talking 1969 to early '70s. One day, my brother and I were coming home, and I had to use the restroom, so we entered a restaurant on the avenue. It looked friendly enough. We had to walk through the bar to get to the restroom. In those days, the rules weren't as strict. Kids were allowed in several places, and everyone smoked in the bars also. It was very smoky, but it wasn't that strange to me and my brother for some reason.

As we both used the bathroom, and on the way out, we noticed something. The bathrooms were all for men—no women. We walked into a gay bar without knowing what it was until we saw people hugging and kissing. We fled out of there to the bus stop. They never said anything to me, but one guy said to my brother, "Hey, big boy." That was my first experience or knowledge of gays.

Several other times, while we'd be standing at the bus stop, things were said very inappropriately to me or my brother. We were never threatened, but we stayed close. One time, I was catching the bus alone, and I hopped on the bus and sat near the back like we'd often do. The bus driver was eyeballing me from the time I got on the bus. Our bus stopped happened to be at the end of the line. That's where the buses would stop for about ten minutes and turn around and start their route back the other way.

On this particular day, I was in the back of the bus and was heading for the front. He did not open the door but fondled me before he would let me pass off the bus. I never told anyone. I thought of many ways to avoid him, but it was the only route and bus available. I would always sit in the back row, putting space between us. It never worked. I was always happy when my brother or someone else who lived near us would ride the route along with me.

It was horrible to be a kid and to have to think and plan ways of escape. I remember even wearing thick tights in hope that he wouldn't be able to touch me. That didn't work either. I wanted it to stop. I wanted to tell, but I was told not to by an adult. Another secret, another violation. Another loss of innocence that no child deserves. Why did they choose me? That was a question I asked myself often. I have never come up with a reasonable answer. I don't know if I ever will.

In between the violations, my brother, a friend, and I had some really good times. Bus fare was cheap on the weekends. An all-day pass cost only one dollar. Movies were fifty cents or a dollar. The music was great. Motown was booming. I loved to dance.

My friends were of all nations—Hawaiian, Native American, Mexican, Caucasian, and African American. I remember the first time I saw a girl wearing a bra. Her name was Darcell. I wanted to copy her, so I went to a thrift store, and with a quarter, I bought a padded bra. My breasts had not yet developed. Most of my family didn't notice, but my oldest sister, Lil, did. She said, "I see you got some bobbies there." I was so embarrassed, and then she started pinching the padding, and we both laughed together. It was after three more years before I truly needed a bra, but oh, well.

I can remember all of us, Shauna and a few friends, all smoking weed under the bridge. We were about thirteen then, and someone got ahold of some malt liquor. It tasted terrible, but we drank it.

It was around that time that I met Chris Vanga. He was fishing with his dad. I had never seen anyone so mean to their kid as Mr. Jackson. Chris and I talked on the phone for a while. One time, my mother and dad left me home, I believe, with my brother, and Chris came over. We thought about having sex, but he was against it, and I was scared anyway, so we never did it. I think I had a crush on him for a year or so. His dad was so violent toward him. He had just one eye because of his violence. I remember him having a glass eye. His two eye colors did not match.

CHAPTER 14

Seventh grade was hard because they bused my brother and me out to the north end to integrate the schools. I never did understand it. It only made me have to walk over a mile to the bus early in the morning. My brother and I would get up before dawn and trudge our way through a mile-length tunnel over several hills to a bus stop right in front of our aunt's house—only to travel another thirty or forty miles by bus out to Ninetieth Avenue to go to school. It was devastating, especially because all my friends from elementary went to Asa Mercer.

I found out that one block to the south divided the different school systems, and I happened to be on the wrong side to continue school with friends. One good thing was that my brother went with me. Thank God because I didn't know anyone. It was hard enough to go from the top of the school to the bottom, and again, not knowing anyone made it difficult.

I'll never forget the loneliness, and the kids picked and teased me because my hair was natural. I didn't make many friends. We all really were isolated. We the blacks all sat at one table, and all the rest of the kids surrounded us. We had a bus attendant who stayed with us throughout the day. Basically, she was the only consistent face we knew. The one good thing was that not only were they integrating by race, but they were also integrating handicap kids. That's when I found a friend who was deaf. She taught me how to sign the alphabet and a few others signs.

Seventh grade went by quickly. The summer was busy, and we stayed at the lake. I loved to swim, and Mom allowed us to do so daily contingent on whether we completed housework chores. We now could go with our friends and stay all day until 8:00 p.m. Shauna and I were together every day during the summer except for the two weeks they went to see family in Missoula, Montana. Back then, they gave a lot of house parties and dances at Mount Baker Hall. We'd be allowed to go, and we were dropped off and picked up. Curfew was at midnight on weekends.

Shauna and I did everything together. We were really inseparable.

When the eighth grade started, it was hard because my brother no longer went to school with me. I made a couple of friends. I remember we started an African dance class, and Crystal Baker and I danced in the talent show. That was the first year I actually got in a fight with a white girl and got suspended.

My mom used my aunt's address and transferred me to Meany School. It was so different from anything I knew. The entire school was full of African American. There truly were a lot of angry kids and a lot of poverty-stricken kids. I can remember befriending a girl and going to her house after school. I had never experienced true poverty until I saw her living conditions. She had nothing but a little worn couch in the living room, a mattress on the floor, and no food. I remember feeling sorry for her.

She was very pretty and had long hair, and I think she was probably half-Indian. I had always thought that she made all the boys like her. The girls were jealous of her, and to think she had nothing when she got home. It opened my eyes for sure. It made me thankful.

I also remember being mixed up with a girl whose name was close to mine. Everyone thought I was her. She didn't have a good reputation and was always fighting. Her name was Debbie Withers, and mine was Debbie Willey at the time. I got that straight with her enemies right when I transferred there.

While I was at Meany, I mainly stayed to myself. The kids were a lot rowdier than I was used to. I know now they were suffering because they lacked essentials. There was one guy who used to taunt me. His name was Johnny. I did not know at the time he had a crush on me. He was aggravating and mean to me. I stayed to myself and went to my classes. I think they took it wrong like I was stuck up, but

I wasn't. I was really scared of most of them and just wanted to get to the next grade without difficulty.

My cousin and I were going to attend high school at Lincoln High School together if we showed we could do well. One day, he tried to bully me for my lunch. I told him no, and he told me he was going to get me after school. I remember being so scared and sick to my stomach. He didn't show up, but I faked sick the next day because I was scared to death of him. He never carried out his threat, and I later learned he was attracted to me and mad because he thought I ignored him because I never responded to him. I just went to class because I loved my classes. They had me in a program that they were trying out. It entailed every child working out of a box. The good thing was that you could work as far as you wanted to without interruption or having to wait on the rest of the class, which had been my problem for some time. I had always finished quickly and got bored waiting. So needless to say, this program worked very well for me, and I excelled greatly. For the first time, I got straight As and even got As in attitude, which had not been the case in previous schools.

I'd always gotten good grades but terrible marks in attitude. It was mostly because I was bored. I'd irritate others after I got finished while waiting. It was a great program, and I did well. My mother was happy too. Now my summer was full of track and field. I joined the track team CAYA and was very involved in track and field. I was very quick on the field and most times unbeatable.

The coach, Coach Oliphent, had two daughters Vida and one who ran a long-distance mile and up, which takes a lot of duration and tenacity. I found this out when our coach entered me into an 880-yard race. It was one I had never done. I was a sprinter.

At the time, we needed to fill the holes in several races, and he chose me to enter along with a tall long-legged very sweet girl. She was a distance runner named Glenda. Looking back, I believe that it was one of the hardest races I ever did, next to a 220-yard run. If I remember correctly, I think we placed second and third. I can tell you that the first 440 yards = to one fun lap. I could no longer feel my legs. They felt like jelly. I don't know how I got the energy to kick at the end and place, but I did somehow. It was a great feeling to finish.

The races I was best at were one hundred yards, the anchor relay of 440 yards, and the long jump. Very rarely did I not place first. I received several blue ribbons and trophies. My mom was always at my track meets every weekend. I don't know how she did it with six other kids, but somehow, she always made it. She was also a parent chaperon on bus trips to Canada and Oregon. I can vividly remember her always being somewhere around, encouraging me.

My mother has never been an excitable type of person, but her beautiful smile and gleam present after my wins said a million words.

I can remember one of the few times I did get beat. At one particular time, I lost to a short, stocky muscular girl named Terry Marine. I was so embarrassed and mad. I always was a sore loser. It was mostly because I very rarely lost. Now I knew that losses make you better and keep you on your game. Sometimes they actually help you up your game. Anyway, she beat me at my one-hundred-yard race. I trained so hard after that. Coach Oliphant had always told us to warm up, eat a good hardy meal, and stay loose, but it took me to get beat before I ever listened (by the way, I've always been hardheaded). I worked out and entered a race I didn't normally run.

It was the 220-yard race. It just happened to be my opponent's best race. It's one she prided herself in capitalizing on. I beat her badly. I don't know how I was able to run at almost full speed for a half of lap (220 yards), but I did to beat her and regain my crown.

My coach wasn't surprised. He always believed and taught me that you could train for any race, but it was hard for me to believe. I was very competitive and always liked to be first in most things in my life, which became a major problem later in life. I remember once we couldn't afford track shoes as a team, and we ran in regular tennis shoes. Once there was an all-white team who recognized my speed, and they and the coaches tried to coerce me into joining their team called the Gazelles by telling me they would provide me with real track shoes. I stayed loyal to my black CAYA team and refused. I often wondered how far or how fast I could have been at that time with the proper equipment.

Coach Oliphant eventually was able to purchase us all track shoes, and it really did make a difference. Along with this, we finally had starting blocks as well. This was a good time in my life for a lot of reasons. It kept me busy and out of trouble and gave me opportunities to travel. It gave me and Mom time alone. It helped with the discipline that I needed. It was a great self-esteem builder and kept me healthy and fit.

At this time, I also had an aunt and uncle on my father's side named Aunt Ruby and Uncle JT who lived around the corner from where I ran track at Garfield High. This afforded me an opportunity to meet and interact with her children, my cousins, who I had just been introduced to at that time. I would stop by a lot before and after practice. It was really the only link I had to my father's side of the family. At that time, we had zero relationships; but in passing or occasionally, my uncle, in his drunken stupor, would drive by his house late at night with me accompanying him and hollering for him to come out. It was very awkward at that time, but I'm sure my uncle in his own way really thought he was helping the both of us.

He would call for my dad to come down, and go to the driveway. He'd tell him, "Here's your daughter," and he'd tell us to embrace, and we would. We'd say hi and bye. My uncle and I would zip off back into the night. My uncle Sammy did that on three or four occasions. At that time, it was awkward, but it definitely made me feel good afterward. That's the only interaction we had for years. So I was thankful, and still am, to my uncle.

Now back to my aunt Ruby. She always made sure I felt part of the family. She made her kids show respect and acknowledge me as Kenneth Wayne's kid, which meant the world to me. Up until that time, I was just the kid on the side—the one out of wedlock. They really only had known my father's kids, with whom they were raised. I loved my aunt Ruby, for she always treated me with love.

I found out later in life when I was around forty that she, too, was a victim of the same situation. She was also an outside kid. Her father had had an extramarital affair, and they produced her. She told me that she always felt inadequate. So she understood, and that's why she was so amiable about her family knowing me and acknowledging me. She said she didn't want me to ever feel like she did.

I love Aunt Ruby because of how she treated me. I place her among one of my favorite aunts. Two of her children, David and Yvonne, and I actually became very close and remained that way in our adult years.

My best friend's father used to call me Speedy Butt. He coached Little League Football for years. His daughter and I would walk to the Rainier field house daily. It was really around the age of fifteen when things changed because my best friend Shauna and I would be going to separate schools for all of junior high. Despite this, we would still talk, and I'd go by her home on occasion. It was a drastic change to our relationship.

CHAPTER 15

It was around eighth grade when I met my first real boyfriend, and his name was Jessee. We actually went together for eleven months. He had a cousin named Jathan who was an only child, and he had everything in his room. My cousin Rose-Ethel and I used to spend a lot of time over Jathan's with Jessee. It was at this time that I fell deeply into marijuana. We smoked weed just about every day. I'd have to walk through a mile-long tunnel to go home; that was a trip. Jessee would always walk me to the other side of the tunnel to see me home. We'd stop and kiss, but we never did go all the way.

Debbie Withers, at this time, lived across the street from him. One night, when we were about to go home, my cousin Rose, Jathan, and Jessee were about to walk me to the tunnel. Debby Withers, unknown to me, called herself liking Jessee. So she and her friend came over as we were walking to start something with us. There were several of them. She was trying to pick a fight with me, but I wouldn't bite. She eventually ended up socking me in the mouth and busting my lip, making it swell. I never fought her back. I knew I would have been outnumbered, and that's what they wanted. Jessee and Jathan finally interrupted the situation and walked us home apologetically.

We actually became friends later in life. I was angry at her for a long time. Needless to say, the fact that Jessee didn't defend me and also hadn't informed me of her liking him (I would have been more on the defense had I known) ended our relationship, but not without me crying my eyes out for weeks.

I wasn't willing to deal with him and the girls. There had also been an incident with another girl named Nadine who had confessed to being deeply in love with him. She would even do oral sex on him to get him to like her, which he never did; he used her. Nadine used to write letters page after page, professing her love for him, and at one point, she confronted me as though he was her boyfriend. I should have left him alone then, but he was such a fun person to be around and a great dancer like me. Together, we would be the stars at every dance and house party. We had even started a small dance company where we danced at different schools and functions. Nevertheless, he got out of the boat after a popped lip from Debbie Withers. He ended up going with her for a short time after we broke up. I found out much later that he was bisexual, mostly gay. He ended up living with an older white man who took care of him for years. He regretfully was one of the early bunch of HIV victims who died before the AZT came out.

It was around this time that my older sister Mona conceived a baby by a much older man. They dated for a while.

She and her boyfriend moved in together and were living in a house above Rainier Avenue. I spent most of my weekends over there. I really loved my niece a lot. After all, she was my first one. I spent most of my time there because I had much more freedom and could go to parties on the weekends as long I was back in the house by a decent hour. Glynn had two younger sisters who I began hanging out with Margaret and Debbie, and both of them were adopted, but we all became close because of the relationship between our older siblings.

It was when my mother and stepfather divorced that things really began to go downhill. Prior to that, as I previously stated, we lived a fairly good life. My stepfather was working for an architectural firm, making fairly good money. We never went without anything. There was always food on the table. Now my mom was our sole support system, and we were now being supported by the state and getting our food from food stamps.

We moved into a four-bedroom house on the corner near an alley on Main Street between Jackson Street and Yesler, both of which could be considered red-light areas.

One New Year's Eve, I went out with my sister and her older boyfriend and his friend. It was that evening that I lost my virginity. My sister thought I went to stay with a friend, but I lied and was actually with her boyfriend's friend all night. It was actually a good experience because he was older at about twenty-eight while I was only fifteen going on sixteen. The following morning, my mom and sister were looking for me, and I lied and kept that lie until now. My mom was so angry she grabbed me. I snatched away, and she fell. She was really fed up with my mischievous behavior, and she had a right to be.

I started drinking, smoking weed, and staying out late. I even ran away once with my cousin. She was frustrated. It was around that time she decided to put me into foster care. I can't remember the date, but I just remember it was around Christmas. I don't think she knew what else to do with me. Anyway, I was placed into a temporary home for about a week. Christmas came, and I remember because my mom gave me a lot of gifts, and I remember it was the first time I ever ate a duck. I helped cook it, and I remember it having a lot of grease. It was very tasty. I was trying to be hard, but it was the first time I was ever away from my family on a holiday, let alone on Christmas. I was so sad. Nevertheless, I played hard and remained silent.

I think if I had called home and apologized, my mom would have come and got me, but I didn't. What happened later made me definitely wish I had. When they finally placed me in a permanent foster home, I was placed in a home with a mid-aged woman and her son. At first, it seemed like the perfect family home. She did allow me to cook, which I wasn't allowed to do at home. Her young son was crazy about me. I think he had a crush on me. His name was Jared. I don't remember her name. After I finish this story, you will realize why. She had an older daughter who lived not too far away. She also had a young relative who was close to my age. She was a few years younger. She idolized me and tried to copy everything I did. I wish now I could have been a better example.

At that time, I got kicked out of Lincoln High where my cousin and I finally got to attend school together. It was something we'd always wanted to do. Not good. Neither of us went to class. We used to skip class and go to the pool hall down the street, the restaurants around the corner, and everywhere but to class. It didn't last long, and my mom withdrew me. She told me if I couldn't be responsible, then I would have to go back to junior high (at Lincoln, ninth grade was allowed), so back I went to Sharples. My mom used my cousin's, Geraldine's, address. That's how I was able to get into that school district. I had gotten kicked out of Wilson. I did okay in Meany but was just a troubled teen. So there I was in a foster home with this woman and her son.

I was drinking at school and skipping a lot. My mom didn't know, but she was notified. I believe she was giving the foster mom an opportunity to enforce her own discipline. That didn't happen, so my unruly behaviors continued. I was hanging out with a teenage alcoholic. We used to go steal wine from the grocery store and get drunk. We'd end up in the nurse station or behind the school in the park passed out somewhere.

No matter how sick I got or chances of my foster mom finding out, I still continuously drank. As far as the foster home, it really wasn't too bad. I mostly came home and cooked for her. I remember she loved steak (boiled). That was a first, but she showed me how to cook it for her the way she liked it, and I did. When I wasn't in my room, I was spending time with Jared. On weekends, we'd visit her family. They all were cordial to me, and I was the same with them. My mom had always taught me to have manners, and I did. I think that played negatively sometimes because I really knew how to play the part.

Everyone loved me, but there were two sides to me and many dark secrets. I tried to mask them with drugs, alcohol, and weed at the time, but that would change too. My friends would walk me fairly close to the house about a block and a half away. Then I'd walk home alone the rest of the way. You know I had to play the good girl part. I couldn't be bringing alcoholic teens and weed heads home. As a matter of fact, I don't remember ever bringing anyone to the house. The reasons were that I was ashamed of being placed in foster care in the first place, and the other was that I didn't want my foster mother to know the crowd I ran with.

Well, you know there are always nosy neighbors, and someone finally told her about my partners in crime and how far they walked me and came home alone. She questioned me about it, and I told her some story about how they lived near and that they were okay. But my mom, unknown to me, was told about my absences in class as well. She put it all together and concluded I was a liar and a sneak and had been pretending to be Ms. Goody-Two-Shoes in front of her and her family when, in reality, the opposite was true. I was skipping school, running with friends, drinking, and smoking weed and cigarettes. She was livid, and she had the right to be, but what happened the next day was one of the scariest days of my life.

After she fussed and told me I wasn't who I was acting to be and gave me her lecture, the next morning, I woke up to a person I had not seen before. It was my foster mom, but I didn't know her. She woke me up and began accusing me of sleeping with her boyfriend— one she did not have. She started calling me a liar and insisted I was sleeping with this unknown man. She began yelling so loud she woke up Jared.

He came out of his room to see what all the yelling was about, and then she accused him of being part of the plot. She said he knew about it too. Now keep in mind that he's only eight years old. I realized then she had snapped, and I grabbed Jared and placed him behind me. Out of nowhere, she pulled out a gun and began threatening us both. I thought quickly and tried to keep her calm by recanting all her statements, "No, ma'am, that's not true. This is your son. There is no boyfriend. You're confused. Stay calm," all while I was moving both Jared and me toward the door. She never took her eyes off us, and I could just think of getting out that door.

Somehow, I got my hand behind me while she was in her raging, "You're a liar fit." I told Jared to run, and both of us ran down the rocks and across the street while she came out into the yard, chasing us with a gun in hand. We made it to the neighbors where I called my mom, and she called the police. My mom came and got me. I think Jared's sister came and got him. They took her to the mental hospital in Western State. After further investigation, my mom found out she'd had had breakdowns before, and the state knew she was unstable. It took me a while to get over that, but it didn't stop my bad behaviors for long.

CHAPTER 16

One night, my cousin and I hitched a ride with a guy who offered us some weed, and he ended up taking us thirty miles away to an abandoned house in the middle of the night and attempted to rape both of us on a bed without a mattress. Somehow, we fought him off and escaped. We had to call home, and my mom, uncle, dad, and aunt had to pick us up. They were so angry. We could have been killed. My cousin and I stayed on restriction. We were either late coming in or not coming in.

One night, I remember sneaking out, and the window was locked when I got home. I couldn't get in. Trouble with a *T.* Restriction usually lasted for two weeks. My cousin and I had gotten so slick that we would plan to get on restriction by staying out late at one party knowing the next party wasn't until the week later. Mom finally caught on and started putting us on opposite weekends. That ended that plan. My cousin was going out with a guy named Sam, and they were having sex. She ended up pregnant at fourteen years old, but she lost the baby. He had a friend named Roscoe, and we were just that—friends. We'd all ride together to parties. We thought we were so cool. We were no longer riding the bus or walking but riding. I remember one of Sam's friends named Marcus picking us up in a nice white car. He had on gloves, but I never thought anything of it. We rode all around the city, not knowing at that time we were in a stolen car. I had no idea.

By now, as you can see, the thoughts of being a track star had gone out the window.

This guy Sam was trouble. He had a baby with a girl named Gerline, and she still cared about him. One morning after we had been out on one of our all-nighters, we ran into Gerline. She told Sam she needed a ride. I didn't trust her, but Roscoe and I scooted over. Sam and Rose were in the front. We stopped at a corner store. She had one tear coming down her cheek. Out of nowhere, she came up with a coke bottle, cracked Rose over the head into unconsciousness, and ran. I screamed. I really thought she was dead. She came to and was fine, but that was scary.

One night, we decided we would run away. Rose and I had no clothes or food, and Sam's friend, a girl, didn't have much either. I remember counting change to get some penny candy. We were so hungry. Friday came, and the young lady whose house we were staying at threw a party. We borrowed some clothes from her, and there we were partying away. My godbrother Derek showed up looking like Shaft—the actor of a well-known movie actor at the time—with a black coat, black pants and shirt, and black umbrella (he's always liked the movies and characters) along with my stepfather and the police. What a scene.

I was scared to death. I was fighting and slipped out of the cuffs. Eventually, they contained us, broke up the entire party (we'd been gone three days), and took us both to juvenile. (We found out later that Derek had squealed. "For our safety," he'd said). Our moms wouldn't let both of us stay and thought we'd have too much fun. I went home. It warranted a month's restriction. I was told by Rose that she did have fun. Her punishment was over in two days once she got out. It was around that time that I started taking Valiums—5 mg and 10 mg actually. My aunt used to take them for sleep, and we'd steal them, and then we started buying them. I can remember taking two or three at a time along with alcohol and weed. It's amazing what the body can take. Or I guess it wasn't my time.

By this time, I was really getting out of hand. I was searching for pain relief—something that could erase how I felt rejected by my biological father. I felt dirty having been molested then by three grown men—one being my stepfather whom I considered my dad. And I felt angry because I didn't know what to do with all the hurt, and I was disappointed in myself for giving my mom so much grief and now really going down the wrong path.

Shortly around that time, my dad and mom got a divorce.

My sisters and brother and I had all confirmed what was an ugly secret. My dad, during his supposed-to-be talks, had tried to touch each one of us. Mom was more than angry. She wanted to kill him, but instead, she left him. I knew it sounds crazy, but I didn't want to leave. I had pretty much grown up in that house off the lake. It was all I had known. It was sad, and so was the situation. My mom didn't have a choice. She tried to talk my stepdad into letting her buy and keep the house, but he wouldn't. He was so arrogant about the whole thing. He did what a lot of people do when they're in the wrong—try turning it on the victims. My mom wasn't having it. That, I believe, was the second time that I had seen my mother cry. The first was when she lost her father to a sudden heart failure. My mom was and is a very strong woman.

My stepdad did her so wrong after all those years together. As a biracial marriage, he played the race card in court. He painted my mom to be an angry, out-of-control poor black ignorant woman. He used his color position and intellect to downgrade my mother in court. My mother's IQ is equal to his, mind you. The judge ended up giving his two kids to him. It was the third time I saw my mom cry. Never mind, he was a reported molester. It nearly broke her heart. She kept her head up and kept pushing.

Somehow, she came up with the money to rent the house on Main Street. My mom, brother Joey, and little sister Jeanette all moved over to what they called then the CD (central district). It was quite a change from the house on the lake.

When we first pulled up, I was so disappointed. The house really needed work on the outside. It did have a nice backyard though (side yard, rather). The inside was okay. We each had our own bedroom. Mom made what should have been the dining room into her bedroom on the main floor.

Since we were now in another district, I had to use our old address after surviving the near-death experience with the long foster mom. I had managed to graduate junior high and was attending

Franklin High School which didn't last long. I quickly got into a fight with a girl named Kim with a huge four-inch mole on her face and was suspended. That put me in the area school district called Garfield High, which was Franklin's rival. Imagine that.

It really wasn't too bad at Garfield. I did try track for a little while again but didn't stay in it long. I was too busy partying, drinking, smoking weed, and popping pills. I did manage to continue African dancing. We'd often go into the federal prison to perform. It was there at fifteen years old that I had my first prison relationship. It was nothing sexual. There was no contact because we were all underage performers. He did write these long intense letters with beautiful handwriting. I was actually flattered, but my mom quickly put a stop to that. He was probably twice my age, and I believe now, knowing what I know, that he was probably an old pimp.

He used to walk me around the facility, showing me off to all the other inmates. He always had a fancy cane, but he didn't limp. He walked a pimp walk with a long stride. That adventure came to an end quickly after I had met a new friend from California and her huge family named the Walkers. The Walkers moved from California. In there were the mom and dad, Sister Lucy and her two kids Ernestein Yolonda and Joyce Shirley, and a young brother named Donnie.

Keep in mind that California was much quicker than Seattle. So they were moving quickly. I befriended Yolonda right away. She was tall, long legged, and beautiful. She was about a year younger than me. She started coming by every day, and we'd hang out. Back then, we looked older, and they didn't care (or ask for ID), so we were able to go into a lot of the taverns and neighborhood bars.

One day, Yolonda and I were in the window and dancing. I noticed the house across the street had a high number of visitors and cars. I never had noticed who lived there though. There was someone who began parking in front of the house because you could not park on the other side of the street, but as I said, I never paid much attention to them.

Yolonda and I were too busy walking looking cute and going out, but on this particular day, we both were dancing in the big-picture window, and I saw him—Eric Barnett. Oh, my, I thought he was the finest thing ever born. It was then that Yolonda and I made a pack.

Our pack was that we were going to walk out when he approached his car and make him notice us, and whoever he spoke to first would be considered lucky, and the other one was out of luck. That's exactly what we did. We pranced ourselves right out the door when we saw him coming down the stairs to his car, and it worked. He noticed us and asked if we needed a ride. It was still an open game at that point, but when he asked me to sit in front with him, all chances were over for Yolonda. *He had made his choice*, we thought.

From that day on, he would stop by every evening. I was still in school (I was fifteen) during the day. He was nineteen at the time and a dropout, drug dealer, user, and thief. (I didn't know or have the slightest clue. All I knew was that I fell head over heels for him.) He'd come by about 8:00 p.m., and he'd have to sit on the opposite couch from me in the living room. Mom's room was right there. She'd have her bedroom door open, watching us for the entire hour. He could stay up to 9:00 p.m. only. I thought he was sleepy, but he was high off of heroin I found out much later.

He always had little burn holes in his clothes, especially his shirts. I thought he must smoke a lot of seed-filled weed. (At the time, weed had a lot of seeds.) I found out later that he had been high off heroin; that's why he was nodding and dropping hot ashes onto his clothing, but I didn't have a clue. I just knew he was cute, funny, and nice to me. I thought, *He'll tell me he is crazy about me too.* And we agreed that when and if we got married, it would be to each other. Big mistake.

He'd take me for rides in the blue and white Skylark, and I'd just be in seventh heaven. I always did wonder why so many people came by his mom's house and only stopped for minutes at a time; they were all copping drugs. I never knew he was a heroin user and dealer. There seemed to be several different types of people living at his mother's house. I never asked him about them though.

There was one guy for sure, and his name was Joe. He was definitely gay. There was another lady who had a few small children. She was attractive, and her name, which I later found out, was Brenda, a cousin of Eric. Unlike Joe, who really was found to be like a brother to him. Then there was also someone living there who was a tall, very unattractive mannish-looking woman. I believe her name was Sandra. His mom and her three youngest children also lived there.

It was one busy house.

I used to sit in the window after school for hours and just watch cars pull up. Most of them were Cadillacs, Lincolns, and a few older cars. Someone would run out, talk to them, and lean in the window, and then shortly after only a few minutes of talking, they'd pull off. I'd watch in amazement. It was like a live movie. I was so enthralled I'd wait anxiously for him to come over every night, and we could speak in an "I-love-you–I-love-you-too moment without anyone hearing us.

One day, I got the nerve to walk over to the house and knock on the door. After all, I thought, *This is my boyfriend.* Boy, was I in for a big surprise. A six-feet-four-inch man-looking woman came to the door and asked me who I was and what I wanted. I politely (though my knees are now shaking) told her I was looking for Eric. Something told me that she was his woman. She didn't know why I was coming to see her man and then proceeded to tell me that I had better never knock on that door ever again looking for her man, or she'd beat me to death. I believed every word she said. I retreated off the porch and ran like the wind back across the street to my house, where I began to cry my eyes out.

My heart was broken, and my world was shattered. I couldn't believe she'd talked to me like that. Could that ferocious thing really be his woman? I couldn't figure it out, especially when he told me every evening he loved me.

My cousin came over, and I told her the entire story. I was so hurt and depressed I didn't know what to do. My world had been crushed by the thing at the door. My cousin and I somehow ended up on the bus. I cried the entire time, vowing I'd now have to end it all (a true teenager). I stepped off the curb, looked both ways (saw no cars, mind you), and lay down in the middle of a two-way street. My cousin was screaming, pulling me up. I was crying my eyes out. I had never been so hurt. I finally got up when I saw cars coming, and she and I resumed our travel. We laugh about it now, but at the time, it seemed like the only thing to do.

When I got home later that evening, Eric came by like he always did at 8:00 p.m., smiling and smoking (and lying). I told him what happened. He was infuriated and told me she was lying and that she was nothing to him. She'd liked him, but he cared nothing for her, he said (liar, liar pants on fire). He said he was going over immediately and straighten her out, which he did because she never said anything to me ever again. She would just stare.

I found out later that Eric was a big liar. Had I known, I would have run far away from him as I could get, but I didn't. I was young and "in love."

Eric took me on many excursions with him, several of which, unknown to me, were burglaries. I had no idea I was just riding along with my boyfriend in seventh heaven. He was so fine. Once, he took me to some apartments. He parked the car in the parking lot and told me to wait and they'd be right back. I heard an alarm go off and saw them come running. I had no clue how to put them both together. They were the cause of the alarms. Both being burglars, I could have gotten a lot of time had they been caught. I could have even be known as an accessory.

Another incident was when we were in the house, and he had me take two small balloons down to his sister who was parked in front of the house waiting. I never knew that it was heroin I was passing to her. He never told me either. I figured it out much later. He took me with him to a couple of joyrides. I was so naive it's almost unbelievable. Yes, I smoked weed, drank, and took some Valium or two. I knew nothing about the hard stuff or the fast life other than what I watched in the movies.

I was about to grow up quickly and find out. Over in the CD or Central District was a whole new life.

Yolanda and I were still hanging out too.

CHAPTER 17

One day, Eric disappeared. I had no clue why. I was told by his mom that he was locked up. I couldn't understand why. What could he have possibly done? I was crushed. I truly thought I had met the man of my dreams and that we would get married when I was old enough and live happily ever after with him. What a joke.

It didn't take me very long to get back up and running. I started hanging out outside of the taverns with much older men, drinking hard liquor on an almost daily basis. My mom was in school and busy, so I don't believe she had a clue about all I was doing. I actually slept with a couple of those old men three times my age. They began to do me favors like alcohol, a few dollars here or there, or a meal here or there at a local restaurant.

I can remember one day I was walking, and a guy in an off-white Mustang picked me up and asked if I wanted to come to his house and smoke some weed. I accompanied him to his apartment, which was right around the corner. I saw him in the neighborhood on several occasions, and he seemed okay. I was to find out differently. He did get me nice and high on weed only. That was fine, and we were laughing and talking. The problem came in when I said I was ready to go home. That's when things changed. He became very persistent about us having sexual relations which I did not want because I did not know him. He, without a weapon, basically forced me to undress and would not let me leave until he satisfied himself on me several times.

When he finally allowed me up and dropped me off, I felt so dirty and wanted to tell someone, but I thought that, somehow, I had led him on and was responsible for some of what had taken place. I now know that a person has the right to say no, and *no* means *no*. That was my first personal experience with a date rape.

Another incident happened when I got in the car for a ride with what I thought was one of Eric's friends. I saw him and Eric together on numerous occasions. I felt somewhat safe getting a ride from him. I thought he knew and respected the fact that I was Eric's girl—not a chance. He ended up taking me to an unknown location where he had me get out of the car, and he tried to remove my pants and panties and commenced to do oral sex on me. I fought him off and ended up getting away and walking home. I'd never even attempted to have it done to me or vice versa. I was totally humiliated and disgusted.

Because I was young and shapely, it seemed I had the word *victim* written across my head. I was approached, it seemed like, daily by men of all ages.

On my way to school in the morning, there was an older man in a big car who used to pull up beside me and follow me and offer me money—fifty dollars to be exact. I'd try to go different ways and leave early, but no matter what I did, he'd seem to ride up on me and solicit me almost daily. I just wanted to get to school. It was around that time that I started going out to a downtown club called John John's even though I was underage. They very seldom carded people.

My sister, cousins, and I would go there nearly every week. We'd also go to Portland on the weekends sometimes and go to clubs. I had an older cousin there who had an apartment with her boyfriend. Going to concerts, clubs, and taverns and drinking were pretty much my life. Eric was still locked up. I couldn't wait for him to get out. I was young and hot to trot. When I turned sixteen in April, I was going to school, but during weekends and after school, I was living the life of an adult for the most part.

In June 1974, there was an end-of-school house party. That night changed my entire life. I ran into Howard Black at the party. He was someone I had had a silent crush on for a long time since elementary. He talked me into leaving the party early and going to his house (his mom's house rather). We snuck up the stairs to his room. It was that night that we conceived the only child I have—a daughter.

I knew, somehow, the next day that I was pregnant. I don't know how to explain it, but I just felt different. I never told anyone, not even him or my mom—no one. I worked a summer job all that summer in Sand Point. I was sick every morning and I had to ride the bus for two hours. I was tired all the time. I'd come home and sleep.

I can remember my breast getting heavier and that knot in my stomach growing, but I refused to believe it, and I really didn't have enough information to know for sure. I was devastated. It wasn't until my breasts actually started leaking milk that I went to my mother and asked her to take me to the hospital. She did, and the doctor pronounced I wasn't dying of cancer like I thought. I was twenty-two weeks pregnant. My mom looked at me and said she knew.

I just wanted an abortion. I didn't feel like I was adult enough or ready to have a child. When the doctor told my mom that I'd have a fifty-fifty chance of survival if it was attempted, that was the end of that conversation. I remember just feeling numb. *A baby? Me having a baby?* I was really nothing more than a child myself. I just cried just about every day for the rest of the term. It seemed that I had just about every complaint a pregnant woman could have—swollen feet, back hurting, and huge weight gain. It was not a pleasant pregnancy.

I had to leave Garfield and go to another school called Washington that had been set aside for pregnant students. I actually did very well, grade-wise. I continued to work after school at a day care near the community college. It was at this school that I met my longtime friend and new BFF Jennifer Miller. Jeanne was due in November with a daughter, and I was due on March 1. We had a lot in common, and we grew close quickly. Ironically, my friend Yolonda was pregnant too just a few months behind me. I never was honest with anyone about who fathered my baby. I was so embarrassed and fearful. It was a hard thing to go through alone, but that's the path I chose.

I can remember being chosen to go to the University of Washington to speak about teenage pregnancy, and I kept my story about who the father of my child was a secret. I really wish in retrospect that I had let him be a part of the pregnancy. It wasn't until she was about six months that I ran into him at Seward Park and told him. He rejected her and said she was not, and I never went to his mother or an older person to announce her arrival or even let them know about her. They formally met her when she was around fourteen. It was one of my biggest regrets ever.

Anyway, back to my story.

During most of my pregnancy, I stayed close to home. All the negative behaviors I had acquired were put on hold. Thank God because she was born healthy on March 2, 1975, early in the evening, weighing nine pounds and six ounces. She was so beautiful with her soft black curly hair and her deep cleft in her chin like Kirk Douglas she actually inherited from her father's father. People came from all around the hospital to see her. She was gorgeous and still is. At that time, all the babies were kept in the nursery except for feeding times. Everyone was allowed from anywhere to view the babies through the glass.

My mother is old-fashioned and insisted I stay home for at least six weeks. She wrapped my breast and stomach with torn sheets and would not let me or the baby leave the house until her six weeks checkup. I'm really glad now that she did because I never had the female problem that a lot of my friends who jumped right up and out after birthing had.

Motherhood didn't come easy for me. At that time, there were no Pampers, and plastic bottles were out of the question. My mom only allowed me to use glass so that they could be properly sterilized. As I stated earlier, Mom was old-fashioned, and even though I was a mother, I was still a teen and still in her house with her rules.

Her rule was that there should be no plastic or anything. This meant resorting to not only washing but also sterilizing each bottle, which meant big pots with boiling water, cloth diapers dipped for BMs in the toilet, and wet diapers washed with Dreft and folded daily. There was no microwave, but I was lucky enough to finally obtain a bottle warmer for bedside for her midnight and 2:00 a.m. feedings. Thank God.

I know it sounds strange, but somehow, I knew immediately in those six weeks at home that I was not the kind to bear multiple children. My mother and her mother were very good at it. Granny bore thirteen, and my mom raised seven herself—with minimum complaints.

As a matter of fact, I can't ever remember her complaining about us. My mom said the same thing about her mother as well. That was not my story. It was always a challenge for me, especially the 2:00 a.m. feedings. She got colic too. So she never seemed to stop crying. I remember one night waking up and just wanting to shake her. Instead, I brought her to my mother, pleading she keep her with her that night. I knew then that postpartum stories were very true. I loved her during the day, and for the most part, she was like my baby doll. I changed her five times a day. She had so many clothes. I'm truly glad my mom made me stay home because I never would have on my own. I was young and ready to get back in the mix. It gave us time to bond, I believe.

Teen motherhood wasn't easy for me. Every morning, I'd have to get myself and the infant ready for school. I was blessed to attend the pregnancy school that had a day care in it. I'd drop her off there and would go attend classes. I was able to check on her during lunch if I wanted to. I did occasionally. I actually did very well in school until the end of the school year. I had met a girl. She was pregnant too, a few months ahead of me. We met and clicked right away.

Unfortunately, we both had lived quite a life before pregnancy, and we both wanted to get back to it—and we did. The street where I usually hung out for the past year was on the way to school, and there was another hot area right to the north. Jeanne and I headed north during school, skipping classes and wandering the streets. I can remember getting back too late to the daycare, and they had called my mom to come and pick her up.

My mom was furious. Rightfully so. My mom insisted I do the mothering. She was not about to become a babysitter, but I found one. There was a lady named Nicey. I sometimes hung out at her house while I was pregnant, and she was pregnant as well. She was older and a lot more stable than me. She really loved kids and was a great mom. Boy, did I take advantage of that.

My daughter was with hers, just about every weekend while I was right back to my old antics. I was in and out of bars and cars. It was around that time that I started dabbling in prostitution on that street just north of the school. That street actually was called Yesler, and it ran east and west one block over from my house as well.

It was around that time that I started running with Yolanda again. By this time, we'd both had our children.

I really liked her family, and they liked me. She had older and younger sisters, and her mom and dad were great people. One of her sisters was Joyce the Juice Walker, the first lady Globetrotter. She was always around my house. She was almost like a little sister to me. She made us all really proud with her amazing basketball skills. Had there been a pro-women's team, she'd have been one of them on the team definitely.

Back to Yolanda and me though. We were moving way too fast, hanging out in clubs for twenty-one and older, and I was just seventeen, and she was a year younger than me. We were in taverns and bars along Jackson and Yesler. One night, we were outside the club "John John's" and decided to sell ourselves for money. To our dismay, we had solicited undercover police. We were underage, so he took us to juvenile. Neither of us got booked. They just called our parents. My mom came and got me. We lied and said he'd trapped us. I don't know if she believed us or not, but we were free.

That was the beginning of prostitution for me. Where I was just drinking and eating with the older guys before, I now started getting money from them, which called for more on my part. A lot of those men were old enough to be my grandfather. Once I started drinking with them, I got the courage to step on Yesler and officially turn tricks. I didn't really have a clue what to do or what to say. I can't remember the first one. I just know I was always drinking beforehand. I was young and beautiful, and it didn't take me long to get the hang of it. Before I knew it, I was filling a jar up on top of my dresser with twenty-dollar bills. I remember telling and showing Yolanda and her taking some of the money. I couldn't prove, it but she was the only one there who knew about it.

Our babies were born in March. Schools were out, and summertime brought on a whole new life. The babies are now four and five months.

CHAPTER 18

I was using Nicey almost daily to get out. I'm paying her, so it was no problem. She was very trustable.

Yolonda had a sister named Ernestine, and we got along well too. She was a year older than me but sharp. She had friends in all kinds of places. It was her who introduced me one evening to Richard at John John's. I was so enthralled by him. He was much older than me, but I attracted him for some reason. The first night that I got into his car, he placed me in the front seat. I was hooked. He dropped Ernestine off and proceeded to his house. His house to me was amazing. He had crushed velvet furniture (that was in back then) and mirrors on the walls and on the ceilings.

He offered me something to drink, and then he disappeared into a back bedroom. I sat there waiting for him to come back out, and he never did. The silence was uncomfortable for a while. Finally, I heard him call me to the back. I got up and walked back there, and he was in bed naked and invited me to join him. I refused. I don't know why I just felt uncomfortable. I could tell he got angry. but he did drive me back home. I was living with my mom, and I was glad. There was something frightening about him, and I just couldn't put my finger on it because I was still quite naive. That was the last time I saw him for a while.

Yolonda and I had started turning tricks regularly. She had Marvin to support, and I had Yona—these were our excuses.

Around this time, my god sister Sharon came around from Alaska. She was a very active prostitute. She worked the streets and massage parlors. She was barely sixteen years old. I remember her taking some muscle relaxers a guy gave her, and I had to rescue her. At another time, she had sex in my bed at my mom's house, and I couldn't wake either of them up. My godbrother and I had to put ammonia under their noses; that's the only way we could wake them up before my mom came home.

One time, she and I were out and got a ride from a guy. The guy ended up taking us to his house to listen to music and smoke some weed. He ended up being Jimi Craven a close cousin. Thank God nothing got started. He died a week later. They found him shot in the park. He had been involved in a lot of criminal behaviors.

I had a friend named Patty who I met when I was back in the ninth grade at Sharples. She actually went with our African drama ensemble teacher. She looked young but was three years older than me. She was also Caucasian and had had a pretty rough raising. She had also been molested and raped by her stepfather, and one of the rapes ended in pregnancy. So she had her stepfather's child. which caused conflict between her and her mom.

For some reason, we hit it off. She had long broken up with the dance instructor. She had moved into a house right down the street from guess who? Richard. Needless to say, I used her location to have the opportunity to walk past his house regularly. I was afraid of him but infatuated too.

One day, he saw me and came out, snatched me into his house, yelled at me, and told me to get seven hundred dollars choosing money immediately. Then he kicked me in the butt and sent me out the door. I went down to Patti's scared. That was serious. Back in those days, girls came up dead all the time. They were snatched and forced to go on the streets. A cousin of mine was found dead, cut up, and stuffed in a gunny sack. I really had acted tough in front of him, but I was shaking going down the street. I really didn't know what to do. This man was obviously a professional pimp.

I'd figure that out. I really felt like I had stepped out of my boundaries I didn't know what he might do to me. It was probably a month later when I ran into Richard again in downtown Seattle at the popular club John John's. I believe we went out to eat once, and the next time was around August when we ended up getting a motel for the evening. I remember that day because it was the day my uncle was honored and inducted as the first black mayor of Washington state. I missed the entire ceremony since I was with Richard. I don't even remember who kept my daughter. I'm sure my mother made arrangements.

It wasn't long after that that Richard asked me to go out of town with him for the weekend. I really truly thought it was a romantic trip. He stated he'd pay the babysitter generously when I found one. Usually, Bernice would watch my daughter for me.

I can't remember why she didn't at that time, but I did get Yolonda's older sister Lucy to agree to watch her for the weekend. I'd spent a lot of time over the Walkers, and I knew the parents Mr. and Mrs. Walker would be there along with Yolonda, her baby, and many siblings. I felt very comfortable leaving her there. I had a few dollars stashed away. So I was sure I'd pay if there were any payment problems. I packed a three-day supply of diapers, bottles, and clothing for my daughter, and off we went.

As he hit the road, the first stop we had was when we checked the tires and got an oil change. He asked if I had money. I told him I had a one-hundred-dollar bill and some change. He asked if he could he have it, so I said sure. I thought truly it was somehow going toward our weekend. I truly was naive and was just feeling like a star being with this older guy in his big beautiful car. It was a new gold-and-white Cadillac Eldorado with a white tire cap on the back. I was really starstruck. I didn't have a clue about what he was really up to.

The next thing he did was hit the freeway going east. I knew that because it was the same way I had traveled when going to my granny's house. I was a little bewildered, but I didn't say anything, still thinking we were off for a wonderful weekend. Boy, was I in for a shock.

He really didn't talk much as he was driving. He did keep making a clicking noise with his throat. I couldn't figure out why he was doing that. I never asked. I found out later that it was how he would scratch the back of his throat. *Weird*, I thought.

It seemed like we drove for hours. We did drive for three and a half hours. I still had no idea where we were going, and I never asked. There was just an eight-track tape playing and an eerie silence. Nightfall came, and we were still driving.

We finally exited the freeway, and the next thing I saw was just lights. Just a long strip of motels and lodges that seemed like miles. I'm sure it wasn't, but to me, it certainly seemed like Hollywood or Las Vegas. It was so lit up. We drove down that road for a while, and what happened next baffled me. He pulled up to a small pool hall and told me to stay in the car, and he was in there for about five minutes.

He walked back to the car, not alone but with a tall woman. She was not attractive or unattractive either. They both walked toward the car. She got in the passenger side. It's an Eldorado, so there were only two doors. He slid back in the driver's seat, and she motioned me to scoot over and slid in next to me. We drove off. Nothing was said about who she was or where we were taking her. She certainly had an attitude. I had no idea why. I was totally clueless that this lady was his wife—Mrs. Denise Noble. No idea!

We drove for a while, and he pulled into a motel. I thought we were dropping her off. Still, there's absolute silence. I don't know if they had talked prior to him picking me up, but she definitely was aware of me, but I had no idea who she was or what she was to him. There were no cell phones then, just pay phones and land phones. He pulled in front of a room. He hopped out, and so did she. He motioned for me to come in as well.

Once in the room, he introduced her as Denise. Then he proceeded to tell me that we're in Yakima called Yaki Vegas at the time (remember I said there were many lights) and that he brought me there to prostitute and make him money. I was shocked and scared. I was thinking to myself, *Oh, Lord, what have I gotten myself into?* I didn't say a word. I didn't know what to say. I had basically been conned into thinking I was spending a weekend with him, and he all along had planned to put me out on the streets. Professionally.

Like I had admitted earlier, I had tampered a little bit with it, but now I was being introduced to the true game. Richard made the rules. I wanted to run, but I didn't know where to go. I had no money, and I was almost four hours from home. I was numb. He had me, and he knew it.

I wanted to cry, but I knew at that point it would have done absolutely no good. So I just went along with the game. There was one bed in the room. He slid in the middle, and she got on one side of him, and I was guessing I was to sleep on the floor. He told me to hop in on the other side. I went into the bathroom, took some deep breaths, and told myself I just was going to play along with this game until he brought me back to Seattle then I'd be okay back home at my mom's. I kept telling myself, "I got myself in this. I can get myself out for sure. I'm strong." I slipped into my gown and exited the bathroom and very apprehensively slid onto the other side of the bed and tried to take up as little room as possible. This was her husband who I had slept with a few weeks ago and had romanced me with flowers and lies.

I don't know when I dozed off, but I woke up to screaming and fist fighting. I'm sure it was about me. Now I had never seen a man hit a woman. I had never seen my mom and stepdad have more than a small argument. I was petrified. I hopped up and pulled on some clothes while he bounced her off the walls, hitting her multiple times, knocking her down, and dragging her to the door and to the outside half naked. When I looked outside, there were multiple cars—Cadillacs and Lincolns—and multiple people, but no one intervened.

I hadn't known, but I was at the Maywood Hotel where 100 percent of the guests were pimps and their stables (or women). It was a bad nightmare. I didn't pray out loud, but I prayed to myself, *God, help me.* I thought I'd be next for the beating. I just remained frozen. I wanted to help her so badly, but I didn't know if he had a gun, or if he'd beat me too. They fought for at least a good twenty minutes. He finally spoke to me and told me to get in the car, which I did in a hurry. He dragged her back inside, and I don't know what happened in there. I was just glad I'd gotten out safely without harm.

If I'd had the keys, I think I would have driven off, but I just sat hoping no one died. I really thought it was possible, especially the way he was beating her. About ten minutes later, the door flew open, and she came running out with the car keys in hand. I looked up into the room, and he was sprawled on the floor looking like he was dead.

She jumped behind the wheel of the car and took off. *It's bad enough that she killed him now*, I thought. I'm an accomplice fleeing the scene, but even worse, she was a terrible driver. She couldn't stay within the lines and was hitting her brakes. She finally looked at me and said, "We're going to the pharmacy. He has had a sickle cell attack [which can come from physical stress, I know now], and we have to go get him medicine immediately." I didn't quite understand, but I was relieved he was not dead. I really thought I was going to die during the drive to the pharmacy because of her driving. She was the worst driver I ever rode with in my life.

So we got the medicine and returned to the room. He was okay. The rest of the day was a blur. I can just remember it getting dark and him telling me to get dressed for work. He was taking me out to work the streets. I was glad to be getting out after that fiasco. I told myself while I was out that I would be planning my escape.

That evening was the worst. Though, yes, I had turned a few tricks on Yesler Avenue, never had I seen so many prostitutes in one small radius. There were about three blocks of red-light area, and there had to be five to ten prostitutes lined up and down the street on every corner and in between. At that time, I had never been to Las Vegas, but they called that town Yaki Vegas because of the number of street activities. It was like a small Vegas strip. I was scared and way out of my lane. I had no knowledge of how to compete. I didn't make one dollar, and I was out for about four hours. When Richard came to pick me up, I didn't know what was going to happen to me. I was truly terrified.

When he got me in the car and asked for money, I told him I had made none. To my surprise, he just shook his head and stated, "You got beat, didn't you?" I didn't know what he meant by that at that time. I learned later that it referred to another working girl not giving you the full cut of what you had coming. I didn't understand the lingo. I was just glad he didn't beat me like he had beaten the lady the day before. I was scared, exhausted, and just wanted to go home. I knew he'd have to bring me home. After all, I'd left my child with a friend for only the weekend. I asked myself, *What on earth have I gotten myself into?*

All I knew was that I had gotten myself into this, and now I'd have to get myself out. As I took a shower and quietly climbed into my side of the bed all three of us were sharing, I just prayed, *God, help me.*

Fortunately, I woke up the next morning, and there was no fighting. Thank God! I wanted to call my mom, a friend, or anyone and alert them to what was going on. I missed my daughter. I missed home. I just kept asking myself, *What have I done?* There were no cell phones at that time, only pay phones, and I didn't even have a quarter to call.

Both Richard and the lady were sleeping, and though I was hungry, I didn't dare arouse them. Around checkout time, he woke up and told me to get dressed for work. I had only brought two changes of clothes. I hurriedly got dressed, and he paid rent and took me to the set in midafternoon. I learned later that it was punishment for not making money the previous evening. It was fine with me.

He didn't know how glad I was to get out of that room and away from them for fear of another fight. He left me out all day and night. I was informed later that the day was mostly set apart for the "white girls" and the mixed girls who *flatbacked.* Now mind you, I didn't know what any of these terms meant, but I learned quickly

When you're a "street lady," I guess that's what I was or was becoming. You'd make some money when you are told to, and I did make some, but I don't remember the amount, and he didn't say much about it. I think he was thinking, *She's fresh and new to the game,* so he was giving me a break. I was thinking this is not the weekend I had planned in my mind. I had been tricked into believing it would be him and me in a nice hotel again, making love. Nothing could have been further from the truth.

When Sunday finally came, I can't remember, but I think we left on a Thursday and got there that evening. Friday and Saturday, he had me work. Back then, almost everything was closed on Sundays.

Richard and I pulled off and headed for the highway back to Seattle. I just told myself that I'd made a big mistake with this guy.

This was not what I bargained for and that I'd get my daughter. Somehow, I'd get back in school, and once I got back home, I'd kiss my mother and tell her I wish I would have listened to her the first time he pulled up to the house. She had told me he was trouble. I didn't listen, but I would now.

It's not how the story went.

Yes, he did take me to get my daughter, and I kissed her so hard. He paid Lucy what was promised and a little more. Then he proceeded to take us both around the corner to my house. All I could think was, *Thank you, Lord. I'm home. I survived. I never have to see this crazy eventful violent man again.*

As we approached the house, he stated to me in a very firm voice, "I need you to move in with me." My heart sank because I knew it wasn't a question. It was a demand. I looked at him through fearful eyes, not knowing how to say no without being afraid for my life. I didn't say a word. As we exited the car, he finished his statement. "I'll be back for you tomorrow, so pack your stuff." I didn't speak. I just grabbed my daughter's diaper bag and walked into the house as quickly as I could. I'd made it home in one piece. I'd survived the weekend. I just held my daughter and cried. I was glad there was no one home at that time.

I cried a river. I went to bed with my daughter in my arms and slept soundly. My last thought before I dozed off was, *What am I going to do when tomorrow comes?* It was too much to take in.

The morning came quickly, and I knew I had to make some decisions instantly. He said he'd be back for me the next day.

What am I going to do? I created a mess. I told myself I'd fix it, but I would not drag my daughter into it. That was final. How I was going to get out of what I'd gotten in, I didn't know, but I would. Drudging the long walk downstairs to inform my mom I would be moving and ask her to keep my daughter for an undetermined amount of time was one of the hardest and scariest things I'd ever done. When I told my mom about my decision to move and asked her to keep Tayona, I didn't want to drag her through what I knew would be challenging for me, let alone for a five-month-old child.

She just nodded her head and said, "You've got your mind made up already, and I'll keep her." I was somewhat relieved. My wonderful loving mom had been there through all my ups and downs and now had to watch her daughter make one of the biggest mistakes of her life. I can only imagine what was going through her head as I turned and went up the stairs to pack my belongings. I'm sure she shed a few tears, but I'll never know for sure. My mom was strong. I'd only seen her cry a few times. Once was during the divorce when she lost custody of her two youngest children, my siblings, to an abusive stepfather.

As promised, Richard showed up the next afternoon to pick me up, and I went with him reluctantly to his house. When we entered the house, it was daylight, and I saw things that I had not seen on my two previous trips over. One item stood out—a child's high chair. I thought to myself, *Not only does he have a lady but a baby too.* Wow! One big happy family. The child wasn't there at the time. I believe she was at her aunt's, but she definitely lived there. There was evidence of her throughout the house.

He walked me through the hallway until we came to the second room on the right. He opened the door and matter-of-factly told me, "This will be your room."

As I looked at the room with a twin bed, a small bureau lamp, and a closet, I longed for my large room at home. I began putting my clothes away, and he walked out and closed the door. I cried again. This would be my prison, for how long? I lay across the bed and took a nap. When I woke up, the rest of the happy family was home. He had a two-year-old daughter named Sheron Suzette. She was a busy little bee. It didn't take long for her to warm up to me. Kids had always liked me. I had dreamed of one day becoming a teacher.

She slept in a crib in the room with her father. A few days later Denise came home, the woman I thought was his girlfriend. I'd find out quickly that she was not only his girlfriend, but she was Denise Noble—his wife. No wonder they had been fighting in Yakima. She was sure to inform me that it was not an arranged marriage but one out of pure love. Again, she tried to ensure me that he loved her. I really think she was trying to convince herself of it. I just listened. I didn't really care one way or another. I thought, *They are both crazy.* I was so glad when he said I would be going back to Yakima. I would do anything to get out of that house. It was uncomfortable. She, he, and the baby were in the big room while I was in the small room. I often wondered why she would put up with such a thing. I quickly learned she really didn't have a choice in that matter either.

He met her and turned her out to the streets at a very young age. I believe she was only thirteen or fourteen from what I heard, and she had been with him for her entire teens. She was then nineteen. It was a sad story too. She didn't have a chance at such a young age.

CHAPTER 19

When he brought us back to Yakima, it was now just her and I in a room with two beds. We worked at night and saved our money. He'd come up on the weekends and pick up the cash from both of us. All the girls and guys of the evening stayed close mostly in the Maywood Hotel, which was run by a big fat white guy named George who slept with most of the working girls in exchange for rent. I had been told to go no further than to the office to pay rent or to the pop machine next to the rental office. Denise and I split the rent daily. I understood why he had given those instructions once I started walking and paying rent.

The few guys who stayed during the week (most of the men went back to Seattle and came on weekends) were constantly trying to add more to their stables (get more women). That was their job—collect girls and collect money from the girls. I was told to speak to no males—period. Except for John's (tricks). I did as I was told. Denise went out to work very late, and I always went out early. I understood later that she was a pickpocketer (thief) and me a flat backer (a girl who lies on her back for the money), a trade of which I hadn't yet learned the tricks. I was glad, though, because that gave me time to be myself. I'd catch a cab down to the track (the streets or red-light areas). I'd go to a place where I could go and cop a few pills (reds or valiums) for downers. They helped me perform sex acts that sickened me.

Along with alcohol, I could almost feel nothing. The problem was that I didn't remember a lot either sometimes. It was my life-saver. Remember that I had started taking pills around fifteen in high school, so I was comfortable buying them. I used to cop from an old man called After Hours. He had a small pool hall around the back street, so I was kind of out of the limelight until I could get good and high, and then I'd go make money.

I met a lot of girls; a few I knew from school and the neighborhood. One night, I met a woman who I will never forget. She really made an impact on me. I guess because her story was more painful than mine. I think I liked her because she was so open and honest, and yes, she was living in a worse predicament than myself. Her name was Marie. Marie was a breath of fresh air for me. She was an older, very attractive woman who was one of the first to talk to me, which was surprising because most of the so-called veterans knew Denise (my stable sister, so-called in street lingo alias Richard's wife) and, to remain loyal to her, really didn't acknowledge or befriend me.

Marie stepped out and did. I later realized we had something in common. We had both been tricked, deceived, and lied to about our new relationships with our men. I was so thankful she stepped out of the box and befriended me against everyone's wishes. She really took me under her wing and showed me the *in*s and *out*s of the game. She taught me a lot by double-dating with me. She was the one who introduced stealing extra money versus lying on your back all night. She was good at what she did, and she taught me a lot. She was really sweet. She drank a lot, I'd noticed, but I understood because it's almost impossible to deal with the streets, John's, pimps, other girls, and the police without something in you. She was a lifesaver. I felt so alone and out of place. I knew this couldn't possibly be my destiny. I had such a good start.

Marie's story was told through her eyes. It was a story of love, sadness, and betrayal. She'd fallen in love with a guy named Rick, and he was doing illegal activity. They got busted, and she took the fall and asked him to please take care of her little sister Joyce. Her sad eyes told the story of what happened next. She did her time for two or three years. I can't remember for sure (the drugs and alcohol fog a lot of memories), but anyway, when she got out, she came home to him—only to find out that he took care of her all right.

That her younger sister and her boyfriend, she had done the time for we're now together and had been for a while. It broke her heart. She was in love with him so, she told me. She'd decided to stay with him. So, yes, they both lived in the same house with separate rooms. Thank goodness. She basically told me the sadness came from crying all the time—two sisters sharing a man. I thought I had it bad sharing a women's husband. There's always someone going through a little bit worse stuff than you. We got along well and made money, so it worked.

I would stay in Yakima for about 90 percent of the time. Denise and I would do alternate trips home to Seattle. I was glad. For the most part, I had time to myself and my own space, especially when he started sending Denise to different states. Then I really was on my own until biweekly when he'd come and pick up his money. We'd have sex briefly, and he'd head back to Seattle. Of course, he had to. He was the main caregiver for his two-year-old.

I missed my daughter and my mom, but I kept telling myself, *I'll figure out a way to get out of this mess.*

Richard really started confiding in me about lots of things. One of his main concerns was about Denise and her heroin addiction. I didn't know much about the hard stuff, so I just listened. Basically, he told me that he was really getting tired of it. He said that Denise had overdosed on heroin three times, one very recently. I really think that's why he chose to deal with me.

Maybe he thought it would jar her into straightening up or something. If it was the reason, it didn't work. She continued using. He became more frustrated. He'd had to rescue her from situations all the time. In retrospect, I think they had grown apart. I don't know if it was the drugs, situations, or time, but there was definitely a wedge. That wedge had driven them both into unarranged (if I can use the expression) cheating. I heard from her (Denise) in a warning that Richard had some kind of crush or special liking for a native American girl by the name of Sherri. We both caught him cheating with her, and she left him (Richard) for a while. That didn't last long, though. I understood somewhat why she was upset, but on the other hand, I didn't really agree because she (Denise) was *chippying* (or cheating) with Sherri's father who was one of the biggest dope dealers in Yakima. A mess!

I was stuck in the middle. I'd actually obtained feelings for this guy over time. I know it sounds crazy, but we talked a lot. I felt for him and for Denise too. Odd. I think I'd always been a caregiver. Because of experiencing molestation at a young age, I was excellent at keeping secrets, so I never told him her secrets, and I never told her his.

Richard did everything. It was his policy to let him do the thinking (which never happened with me because he got me older than fourteen), but I let him think that he did. He bought all our clothes, shoes, coats, and boots. All money (he thought) went to him. Then he did the buying and issuing. Denise made a lot more money than I did, so her things were normally nicer or more expensive than mine. I didn't like it, but I accepted it.

Denise was forever doing something to get herself in trouble. For instance, her birthday was on December 19. I was delegated by Richard to do one thing—get her on the Greyhound bus in Yakima—and on the other side in Seattle, Richard and his entourage would be there to greet her and take her home where they would be giving her a birthday bash. She was turning twenty. Well her and her so-called *friend* got into it in the lobby of the hotel while we were waiting on a taxi to take her to the bus. They fought for over half an hour. It was hilarious because they were both loaded (high) and spent, most of the time missing swings at each other. I tried desperately to get her in the cab, which I finally accomplished, and to the bus depot to depart for Seattle. She did make it to the bus and arrived in Seattle, but—wigless (everyone wore wigs), scratched up, and with clothes torn.

When she walked off the bus, that was how Richard and his entourage viewed her. Omissa and her had caught the same bus to Seattle, a three-hour trip, and had fought the entire way back. Richard told me the story with such disgust. As I said, I believe it had been over before I came into the picture. I really think it was the child that kept them together.

CHAPTER 20

My first time flying was going to be to Alaska. At that time, they were putting the pipeline through there, and there was plenty of money.

Alaska was known to be the place of wine, women, and song. I was actually excited because Richard said that he and I would be going together. I looked forward to going out of town for the first time by myself with him.

Denise was in Arizona with some working girls, friends of hers. Another thing is that my godmother had moved to Alaska to work in the canneries, and my god sister Sharon who was also a lady of the night lived not far from where we were going (Fairbanks, Alaska) in Anchorage, Alaska. I heard great things. As I said, I was excited.

When it came time to go to the airport, he made up some excuses and put me on the plane alone I was scared to death. I'd never flown, and I didn't know anyone in Fairbanks at all. He gave me $150, enough for a room and a note that said, "the Flame Restaurant," and left me to travel alone. I really thought about just waiting till he left and getting in a cab and going home to my mother's house, but I didn't. I just sat there, and a woman started talking to me. It ended up that she actually was a relative. She was a Finister—my best cousin's first cousin. As she put it, she was older and more experienced. She had been to Alaska several times and knew her way around.

We had a ball. We drank and made money and clubbed. I, at some point, lost contact with Richard. I didn't care. I couldn't believe he did me like that. He lied and said he was coming with me. I spent money and eventually traveled by plane to Anchorage and caught up with my god sister. We partied there, and I never contacted Richard. I was free—once again. I was living the life of a teenager, having fun, going to concerts, and shopping. I was sending money home to my mother for my daughter for a first. I was living the life and was hundreds of miles away from Richard, Denise, and that craziness. I had what they call in the streets "running off"). I was having a ball.

I met an older man named Burley who was crazy about me and owned a trucking company. He knew I was young, but he didn't care. He was sure he could handle me and make me happy. He began dating me. I started saving money in my suitcase.

He'd given me an extra car so I could get around. One night, one of the Eskimos stole it and took it home. Thankfully, the police found it and gave it back to me.

Burley took me to some of the best restaurants and diners. He paid my rent daily and gave me money whenever I needed it. I ran into this older lady who knew Richard through her man. She was sickly but still working. She didn't make much money, so I kind of let her stay in the room with me. I even turned her on to a couple of tricks, so she could have some money, but she betrayed me. One day as I was approaching the room, I pulled into the parking spot in front of the room. Later that night, my sister and I met at a club to see the famous Platters. I had just arrived back, and there was a knock at the door. I asked who it was. I looked at her, and she had a funny look on her face, and the person on the other side of the door said, "Silky." My heart almost stopped. That was the street name Richard used. He had found me.

I was shaking as I opened the door. He said only two words—"Follow me." I did, and to my aghast, he was in the room right next door. How long had he been there? What had he seen? How did he find me? These were all the questions I asked myself as I walked out my hotel door and entered his. He immediately hit me a couple of times. I protected my face. I really thought he was going to hurt me badly, but he didn't. After he slapped me twice, he stopped. I don't why. It had to be my prayers or the fear in my eyes. I don't know, but he stopped.

I ran into the bathroom and washed my face. When we came out, the first thing he asked was, "Where was the money?" I had been saving some of it. It was in my luggage next door. He let me go get it. When I knocked on the door, the older lady answered with a smile. I knew she had betrayed me.

She was the only one who knew what hotel I was in and what room. But why? I didn't understand. I believe she was jealous because I made a lot more money and was seemingly happy. She always hurt and complained. Anyway, I'll deal with her later. I grabbed the money out of the suitcase and hurriedly went back over to his room. He counted the money and was not happy with the amount. I had been gone for almost a month. He asked me about the amount. I told him I had been sending money to my mom for my daughter (something he had never offered to do). He mumbled something and told me to drop my drawers. (That was his way of saying he wanted sex.) I was stunned.

First of all, I'd never been hit by any man ever. Second, I had been hit, and now he wanted to have sex. It made me sick to my stomach to even think about it. Talk about mixed messages. Anyway, I was on my period, so I thought, *No problem.* To my amazement, he told me he didn't care and to grab a towel. I did as I was told. It was better than getting hit again.

He asked me lots of questions as to why I ran off or hadn't called. He even tried to act like he was concerned. I rattled that I was very angry he had sent me all alone to Alaska. That was not the plan. He made up some lame excuses. I didn't believe him. I just really wanted him to leave. I was hoping he had got what he wanted—the money and would now leave me in peace. I really was truly enjoying my life in Alaska.

Burley asked me to marry him, and I really was considering say-ing yes. He was a very nice guy, and I'd definitely be financially set—with him being the owner of his own trucking company. But my worst fear came true. Richard wanted me back in the states (USA). (Alaska is part of the United States, but they called it the lower United States). He wanted us to leave the next day. I was devastated.

Somehow, I talked him into letting me stay while he went back with a promise that I'd follow him back by the holidays. For the next two weeks, I worked very little. Burley wouldn't let me. He gave me money weekly to send to Richard, and we just spent a lot of time together. He was still considered a John, so money came with the arrangement. He also paid the hotel rent daily. I put the old lady out. I never told her I knew she'd given me up, but she knew why I asked her to leave. I told her some lie. I think Richard probably paid her or something because she went back to the states, I heard. Good riddance!

I thought of all kinds of ways how to stay in Fairbanks, Alaska, but deep down inside, I knew that somehow someway, he'd hunt me down and find me.

I cried all night before I left for the airport, thinking about the jail I was going back to. Richard picked me up from the airport. Before I could even take a breath, he stated he was sending me down to Phoenix where Denise and her friend Carole had been for the last month. They supposedly had been making a lot of money. I was home in the little room for a day or so. I got to see my mom and child for a short time, and off I went to Phoenix, Arizona.

It was my second trip on an airplane alone. I was becoming a pro. As I took off, I ordered a few drinks (of course, with fake ID because I was only seventeen) and thought about a good life short-lived in Fairbanks, Alaska.

When the plane landed, I saw all the beautiful palm trees and the sun setting. I don't think I had ever seen anything as beautiful as this. I gazed out the window almost as if I was in a dream. The Phoenix Airport and the Fairbanks Airport were like a lifetime away. The day I left Fairbanks, the temperature read −50°. It was so cold that the fog had frozen. As I had boarded the plane, they said I was on the last plane to fly out because of the fog freeze.

Now here I was, less than seventy-two hours later, landing in a temperature of nearly 80°. The plane allowed us to exit on the runway. In the midst of the beautiful night air, the beauty was almost unbelievable. It actually looked like a postcard. I was living!

I came back to my senses once I pulled up to the hotel in the cab and knocked on the room door, and Denise answered. Dream over. We'd shared a room before, but there were always her friends around, or Marie would save me from staying too long after awakening with her. We really had never had words or anything. It was just uncomfortable, her being married to the guy I was sleeping with every two days in the same house. It just felt weird.

She opened the door and lay back down on the bed. I was glad because I didn't really feel like talking. I was just taking it all in—just how much my life had changed in six months. Thankfully, we had two beds. So I unpacked and lay across the bed, just gazing out the window. There were orange and lemon trees full of fruits right up against the window. Amazing. I dozed off to sleep for a couple of hours myself.

When I woke up, we both got dressed to go out. It was actually one of the few times we'd worked together. Before going out to the track, she informed me she had to get her fix before going out (her heroin fix). It wasn't the first time she'd informed me of her heroin habit. She once had asked me in Yakima for twenty dollars so she could get fixed at the same time convincing me he wouldn't miss my twenty because he expected more out of her because of her thieving experience. Whatever! I'd given it to her then, and I'd go with her now to get fixed.

I'd always been told she did way too much, and I saw it for myself. She'd be so loaded she'd almost be falling. I didn't know you could hold an entire cigarette that was ashes only between two fingers until I met her. We traveled in a cab to someone's house. I waited while she did her thing (fixed). Then we went off to the streets. The strip at that time was Van Burien Avenue. We took a seat on the stoop. It didn't take us long to catch a couple of Johns, and we went to their hotels. Halfway into the date, she beckoned to me in street language, and I made my way toward the door. That meant she had gotten the money (picked a pocket) while I headed for the bathroom pulling my shirt down and clothes up. I opened the door for her and headed toward the elevator, stating the cab was early, and waited for her to dart onto the elevator.

We managed to get out of the hotel and ran for three blocks and finally made it to our hotel. She had taken about $1,400 from her guy. Now normally with two people, we'd put together all we made and split it down the middle, but since it was all going to Richard, she sent it off in her name only. The next week was slow, and he told us to bring our broke behinds home. Because we didn't have much money, a couple hundred a piece, we were to take the Greyhound.

The week hadn't been as bad as I thought it would be. Denise and I actually had gotten along pretty well. She had told me the story of how she and Richard met and how she was young and rambunctious. She was really nice once I talked and listened to her. Like a little kid in a woman's body, she had never really had the opportunity to have a child's life. She told me how she met him at thirteen or fourteen, and he turned her right out to the streets. She told me he had another woman too when she met him and how they had slept together prior to her actually being with him. Sounds familiar. Anyway, she actually had a friend in Phoenix who had what we called a square boyfriend. He'd picked us up one day and took us horseback riding in the mountain and skating. He belonged to a motorcycle club. He was really nice. His name was Reggie. The ride home on the Greyhound was awful. Denise was dope-sick the entire time. She tried to cop in a couple of states, but she was unsuccessful. She lay across me and on my shoulder the entire three-day trip. I was so glad when we pulled into downtown Seattle.

Richard was there to pick both of us up. He teased and called us broke broads. We laughed it off because we were close to broke.

For some reason, the last week wasn't financially successful for either of us. I was just glad to be back home to my little bedroom and off that Greyhound bus. I vowed I'd never take a trip that long again on it. I haven't.

We got home just in time for Christmas. Christmas had always been my favorite holiday. Everyone was in the holiday spirit. My company was in and out of the house, which I liked because Denise wasn't so pleasant to me in town as she was out of town. I never really figured out if she liked me or not because of that.

She was definitely wishy-washy with that. I made up my mind that I wouldn't let it bother me, but deep down, it did, especially when she confided out of town. She knew exactly when he spent time in the night with me. Funny, he thought she was asleep, I'm sure. Awkward!

Somehow, though, I was getting used to the life. I liked the lights, the cars, and the nightlife. It seemed like everyone in the life had two or more girls.

My god sister shared a house with two other women and her man. They were all given days of the week to spend time with him (true story).

Some of the guys (pimps, let me call them what they were) had up to seven girls. One for each day of the week. I saw it all in Yakima and Alaska, and I was only three months in by this time. I saw whole families march down to public safety buildings and get shot altogether for cases of gonorrhea. I saw quite a lot of lesbianism, which was a first for me. I had known several homosexuals. My play sister would take me to their clubs to dance. That's how I learned to do the hustle dance. It was one of the first black line dances I knew of. The guys were out of town all week, and when the cat was away, the mice will play, and they did. I definitely saw the unmentionables.

Back to the first Christmas. He sent me to Yakima, and Denise and I got home two days before Christmas. She was home and stayed for her birthday on December 20.

During the few days, there was a night when she was sick, and Richard used to snort heroin and coke. He actually introduced them both to me.

Remember I was a pillhead (that was minor stuff). I remember her getting some of his stash and tipping it to the bathroom to get a fix, unbeknownst to him. I never told him anything she did. I think it was because of the early molestation and being told to keep secrets. I had gotten really too good at it. Anyway, I remember her saying it was no good, and she was still sick, but it had taken the edge off.

Remember that this was someone who could do a spoonful alone herself. So she thought that's why I believe she OD'd so many times. I realize now that she was trying to mask and numb the pain of a lifetime of prostitution. She never had an opportunity to be a child, a teen, or a young adult. She'd had to grow up quickly under the hand of a man nearly twice her age. Not making any excuses for her, but it was hard for me at seventeen. I can't imagine going through it at thirteen.

Nevertheless, after eighteen, we're all responsible for our destinies. I just really think she thought she was stuck. I had never heard her say she wanted to do anything else. I never heard her share dreams or visions about a different life. It really was sad watching her get so high. I think I asked her one time why she did. She didn't know why.

We actually had some fun over the holidays. Denise and I went to see the movie *Sparkle* without Richard's consent. Like I said before, he managed just about our every move. He even bought our bras and underwear. So when we snuck off to the movies, and he found out, he was furious. We didn't care. If you've ever seen the movie *Sparkle*, you'd understand why. It's about three sisters who sing, but one gets caught up with a player who beats her and humiliates her constantly. He also feed her drugs until she became an addict. She finally died.

The movie never disclosed the cause of death whether it was from the beatings or the drugs. This all happened against her mother's advice. Sounds familiar again? She could have been Denise or me.

Anyway, he was angry because he controlled us by a lack of information. His favorite line was, "Stop thinking. I'll think for you. Your thinking will only get you in trouble." I never bought into that. Thank God. My mom had always taught me to think for myself. Richard had once slapped a book out of my hand when I was reading, which I did a lot when I was there at the house. I never said a word. When he left my little room, I just continued reading.

He didn't stay mad at us long, but by the next evening, he was mad again. I guess we must have gone to the movies on Friday. I say that because most weekends, Suzette (their child) would go to one of Richard's family members where he'd go to after hours. I think that's how we pulled it off.

Saturday came, and we all went out together for the first time. I remember because the jean outfits that used to be really fancy with suede and leather were popular then. He and Denise wore their fancy ones. He'd bought them both. (I was the new girl, so I got less I guess.) I wore the one I'd had for a while, but it was okay. I was just glad to get out of the house. We all entered the club together, but it wasn't long before Richard found his way to the VIP (pimps' area). They had them in each club in the city. Denise and I sat for a while, but when we both were asked to dance individually, we both accepted and hit the dance floor.

We danced right next to each other. That was a silent code in the street. You stayed with your stable sister and her outings (supposed to be one big happy family). The dance named The Point was out, and boy did we point. Down and up, side to side—we were laughing, dancing, and having fun. Wouldn't you know it, ole grinch Richard returned to the table and found himself womanless for a moment—a moment too long, he figured. I don't remember if he came and got us or if he was waiting when we returned to the table. I do remember he was fuming hot. He told us to follow him, and we did. He marched us right out of the club, just like we had marched in three little ducks in a row. I couldn't understand why he was so mad, but he let me know quickly, or should I say us. Everything was us when we were in Seattle.

He yelled and screamed in the car, demonstrating our dance techniques. He said I was pointing, she was pointing, and the two we were dancing with were pointing. *Okay, what's your point!* He didn't like the fact that we were having fun, especially without him and with someone else. Well, that was just too much for him.

I think we all went to bed without speaking—me to my little room and them to theirs. At least there was no fighting. Before drifting off to sleep, I thought, *It was worth it.* It was fun going out and dancing. He shouldn't have been mad.

After all, he met me in a dancing club. He always told me he loved the blue satin dress I'd had on and matching blue shoes and a blue leather coat. He'd always stated he especially liked my thick legs.

CHAPTER 21

The second time I'd been away from my family on Christmas was in 1975. I missed my mom, sisters, brothers, and especially my daughter. I had only gotten to see her a few times in the four months mostly because I had been out of town. When Richard would take me, he'd drop me for an hour and pick me back up. The other reason is that I really think he didn't want me around my family who loved me and influenced me. It was probably both. At any rate, he did take me over to my mom's on a Christmas afternoon. If you noticed, I stated afternoon. The reason was that the Noble family (that was Richard's last name if you don't remember) had breakfast every year at his grandmother Lonie's house, Richard's mom's mother. His mother, Altine, was a dear heart. She also was an only child. Tine was what everyone called her. She knew my family and was so sweet, educated, and worked for years in the juvenile detention facility, and she was a Christian. Her husband, Richard's father, was the opposite. He ran a pool hall and was more involved in the fast life.

I guess that's where the brother, George, Richard's younger brother, had picked it up. George had at least seven to eight women at one time. The main one was Shirley, who is still with him to this day. I'll get to that later.

Christmas morning came, and Richard, Denise, the child Suzette, and I loaded up. I had no idea where we were going. He seldom told me. Remember that he wanted to be in full control. I just went along with the plan because I knew I'd see my family because he bought and wrapped a large present for Tayona. This meant I'd get to go and drop it by.

I felt so uncomfortable. No one seemed to think it odd that Richard his wife, child, and then me seemed odd. You would have never known.

If they did, none of them acted like it. George and Shirley were there, but none of his harems were with him and his "main woman." I just hadn't been brought up that way. That was one of the hundreds of days that I just wanted to disappear into thin air. Not one of them treated me badly. Lonie loved Richard. She called him Ricki. He was her first grandchild, and I could see they had a close bond. That's why I didn't understand why he brought me along. I knew his mother knew about me, but I wasn't used to meeting an elder, someone's grandmother, in *ménage à trois* form. That wasn't in me. Once again, I said nothing. She had the table laid out with every breakfast food you could think of. Everyone was having the time of their lives. I played the part smiling.

I couldn't wait to get over to my mom's where I thought things were seminormal.

I didn't like disrespecting his grandmother like I felt I was. I couldn't understand why everyone went along with Richard's and his brother's behaviors. I still don't!

I always felt like someone should have said something to them about the pimping, the women, and their lifestyles. I never heard it once from any one of the sisters, brothers, mother, father, or grandmother. Strange. Maybe they had, at one time, said something to them, like my mother had talked to me before I drove off leaving my daughter and hopping in that long Cadillac. But not once did I hear from them. It was interesting because the family all were church-going people.

Getting back to that Christmas morning, after we ate, they visited. They said their goodbyes. Our little family hopped back in the car—Denise in front with Richard, of course, and Suzette, and me in the back. I was kind of starting to get slightly attached to the little girl.

They all dropped me off at my mom's. I was so excited to be spending Christmas with my daughter and family, and I had a gift. I hadn't given my mom much since I'd left Alaska. I always felt bad about that. I gave all my money to Richard to take care of me I suppose. That's his words.

His daughter was well taken care of. Even though I knew my daughter was not lacking anything and that my mom took very good care of her, it still wasn't coming from me, and I always felt bad about it. Later on, I learned to stash (put up money that he didn't know about) money, and I bought things for her (my daughter). As I said, I was just happy to be home. Of course, they'd all open their presents. I was gleaming when I walked in with this huge wrapped box, only to be so disappointed when Tayona unwrapped it. It was a big cheap Caucasian ugly doll at that. It looked like something that had come from Woolworths or Kress store.

No thought was put into it. It was almost taller than Yona, and it scared her. All my family, I could tell, were just as aghast as I was. I wanted to melt into the floor. I felt so bad. I could not believe he did that. I don't know why, but look how he treated me. Duh! After an awkward silence, everyone came to themselves. I know they knew I didn't buy it, but I still felt so bad and humiliated. I guess because I knew he made his daughter's Christmas memorable. She had everything. Why was I allowing this? I vowed to myself that would never happen again.

From then on, all the packages and gifts were handpicked by me, most of which he knew nothing about. I had fun spending time with my daughter and family. It didn't last long. He was back to pick me up in about two hours. Off I went back to Dawson Street (that was the street name of their house).

The unveiling of the evening gift started like the morning breakfast—awkward. He bought both of us a few gifts, and one of her's was a full-length silver-fox coat.

I was insulted (he had gotten me leather), but I didn't show the discontent on my face, and I didn't say a word, but I was fuming. I kept the feelings inside and poured myself some drinks—peppermint schnapps to be exact. After two or three (those sweet drinks sneak up on you), I was drunk. Richard was so angry about it that he took the bottle and slapped me. This was the second time he'd hit me. I was so drunk that I barely felt it. I just lay across my little bed and went to sleep, or should I say I passed out.

The next morning, as usual, he was knocking on the door, which was the ritual. He'd wake Denise and me up. She would clean the living room and dining room. I had been assigned kitchen duty immediately after I had moved in. He liked the way I washed, dried, and put away the dishes and wiped down everything spotlessly (my mama taught me well) as if that was a compliment coming from him. I really didn't know what I saw in him besides his sense of humor. He could be really funny at times. His bedroom skills really weren't over the top, average, I'd say (That was one thing Denise and I agreed on).

When I think back, I think the attraction after a while was that he did take care of everything. I mean, yes, we both went to work and made money and gave it to him. Besides cleaning the house, neither Denise nor I did anything. Richard did the cooking, the washing, and the shopping. He took care of the little girl, and he paid all the bills—mortgage and car note. When I really think about it, he was more like a father figure. But he was an abusive one.

I was actually glad when the holidays ended. That meant I'd be sent back to Yakima. Yeah! He never let us work in Seattle at that time. I went to Yakima, and I believe Denise went to the islands, maybe Barbados, with one of the girls she worked with. That's the way it mostly was back then. Girls teamed up in twos. One of the reasons was for safety purposes. The majority of the reasons were for teamwork on the streets and for stealing.

I was getting better. I'd been taught by some of the best— Denise and her clan. I still didn't have it perfected alone, so a lot of times, I still made money on my back (flat backing, it was called). It wasn't easy work.

CHAPTER 22

When I returned to Yakima, I ran into a girl I'd known or heard of from the old neighborhood in the CD or central district. We got along immediately. At the time, she was with a guy named Tommy. We worked well together, and I liked her a lot. She had a two-year-old daughter with a mutual friend named Spencer. We had that in common, and we knew a lot of the same people. We always made good money together.

She was very thin and pretty. I was size twelve, thick, and pretty. She had little breasts. My breasts were always large. We made the perfect package of choice. If they wanted thin, they'd pick her. Our plot was that you have to take a friend. So they'd take me. If they wanted thick, then they'd have to take her along with me. We used various excuses why and dozens of different names. It became a game of role-playing. It was around that time that I really started getting comfortable with the lifestyle. I was back and forth to Yakima for the next six months.

Once, I was hospitalized for a bad case of gonorrhea. I had such a high temperature that I passed out in my motel room. Thank God I hopped on the bus to Seattle and went straight to the university hospital. I passed out right there at the entrance. When I woke up, they told me I was very lucky to be alive.

My temperature had risen over 105°. I was hospitalized for four days. They treated me with a vigorous antibiotic regimen. Richard came once and brought me flowers.

That didn't slow me down at all. I was right back at it within a week. Prostitution had become my lifestyle.

I stayed in Seattle for a while—unfortunately. I say that because one day, I got mad and left him and that wife in the house. I packed a bag and went to click my heels down Empire Way, the main street by the house. When he discovered I was gone, I was nearing Rainier Avenue. I walked nearly a mile. He pulled up beside me and told me to get in, but he followed beside me for a good while, trying to convince me to hop in. But I said no multiple times. Why I left seemed legitimate to me. I felt I had done nothing wrong. He obviously thought I had. I'll let all of you decide that. So let me tell you what happened that morning around ten.

I was up sitting in the living room, and the phone rang. Denise, Richard, and Suzette were all still in bed asleep, so I thought to answer it. I said hello. There was a woman on the other side. Her voice did not sound familiar. His sisters and friends called frequently. I did what I had always been taught to do. I said hello and asked who was speaking and who would they like to talk to. Well, I guess the lady didn't want to give her name, so she hung up. Now I had no idea who she was, and I really didn't care. There was so much going on all the time I was there. I felt like I had done my secretarial job well. Well, he didn't. I guess the lady was one of his previous girls before Denise or while with Denise. Whatever! But he was fuming mad when she called back and got him on the line.

He came storming out of the room, yelling at me, calling me a bitch. It was something no one had ever called me before. He began lecturing me about who I thought I was, questioning the woman on the line. He proceeded to tell me this was some girl who had been with him for years and knew him and who was I to question her. He said that I should have just given him the phone.

I tried to explain to him that I did not question her but only answered the phone in the correct manner I had been taught. He did not hear me. He just ranted and raved about it. She really must have meant something to him. I didn't really hear anything clearly after he called me out of my name—bitch, a female dog, that I'm not. What was I thinking? I'll show you who's a bitch. I was thinking, not talking.

When he finished his little fit and returned to his room, I went to my room, packed a few things in a bag, and made an exit out the door. He'd slapped me twice, now I'm a bitch. No way my feelings were hurt, and I'd done nothing wrong.

He was doing all that fussing over women who had obviously left him for quite some time. He had a wife and me. *He's crazy*, I thought, as I walked out and quietly closed the front door. Denise stuck her head out the door and asked me where I was going. I just kept walking and stated, "I'm leaving," as if she really cared where I was going. She must have squealed and alerted her husband of my escape attempt. That's how he got to me on Empire before I make it to Rainier.

As he continued to ride alongside me, he asked me why I was so mad. I told him I'd never been called a bitch. I wasn't one and would not tolerate being called one. Imagine that coming from me. I was prostituting for him and sharing a house. Don't call me a bitch! He thought it was funny, me mad and him riding, pleading for me to get in. He finally talked me into the car by telling me he'd drop me off at my mom's if that's where I wanted to go. That's where he dropped me off. I believe I spent that day and night at home.

On the next day, he came with flowers and a card, apologetic. I didn't go back to his house that day; instead, I went to work in Seattle for the first time in six months. I walked down Jackson over two blocks to Yesler and caught a customer (a John) right away and several after. I don't know how he got wind of me being up there because remember he didn't let Denise and I work at Yesler. I always said he had eyes and ears on me everywhere. He coaxed me into the car. I felt like I really had no choice, and he took me back to the house. That's when he realized I could make money in Seattle.

After that, he had me work in Seattle quite a bit. I remember one night shortly after I had started working in Seattle. I'd gotten home and was seated on the couch. He sent Denise out to get my money. (I was furious but too tired to show it.) I gave her the money. She returned shortly to tell me Richard said I did good. The nerve of him! I tolerated it though. That was the one and only time he did that though. Maybe he felt my anger. I don't know, but I was glad. I could not stand Denise when we were home.

Richard found a way to work me six days a week now that I worked in Seattle streets too. Back then, no one worked on Sundays. Things were all closed. That eventually changed though, so I was bounced back and forth from Yakima. I was home for a few days, mostly when Denise was out of town.

I didn't spend much time with my daughter as I said previously other than the occasional drive-bys he let me do to my mom's for an hour.

CHAPTER 23

One day, Bernice, the babysitter for Yona, told me that my daughter was sick. I was in town. She was still occasionally staying with the same friend and sitter (we had both been pregnant). When I got there, she was so frail. She was having diarrhea. She had gone through several diapers that morning. She was about eleven months. She was walking and looked dehydrated. I took her immediately to the children's hospital where she was diagnosed with salmonella. It can occur from bad water or things sitting too long. She was hospitalized for a while. I don't know how long because I left that evening once my mom showed up and came the next day. She had lost so much weight, and I remember her being hooked up to so many tubes. I just cried. It was also at that time they discovered that she was born with just one kidney. The other kidney never grew. It all was too much for me. I ran out of the hospital like Cinderella at midnight and never returned.

As I lay in my motel bed days later, I wondered what kind of mother I was who leaves their kid in the hospital and never goes back. I, once again, took pills and alcohol and went to sleep. I tried desperately to put the sight of her in the hospital bed out of my mind. The drugs and alcohol helped, but they always wear off, and I was left to look at my true self in the mirror.

I called home. My mom informed me that Tayona was out of the hospital and was doing fine. The kid bounced back quickly. Mom said she was running around like normal. I was glad to hear it and slept well that night.

When I arrived in town, I went by to see her and held her real tight. Had I made the right decision to leave her with my mom? That question ate at me for years. After watching so many of the girls drag their kids with them from home to home and motel to motel, I came to a conclusion. It would have been so selfish to take her. I really don't know if my mom would have let me take her over to Dawson Street in that living situation. Anyway, I never asked. The funny thing was that I was around Suzette every day (their daughter) sharing in the care for her, but Richard took very little interest in my child.

I never figured that out, but it used to really bother me. I think he took my daughter one time to the circus, and he complained the whole time about how my mother dressed her and did her hair. (My mother was never the best at hair.) He said it could have been done better, but the complaining took away the enjoyment of the event.

I didn't say a word. I had learned to keep quiet. It's something that was not my normal nature. Once again, the grinch spoiled Christmas oops, I mean the circus. What a grinch.

Once, I thought I was doing both Denise and Richard a favor by taking Suzette to a birthday party—only to get home and over-hear Richard telling Denise about it. Her response was, "I need to be taking my daughter, not her." I thought, *How ungrateful*, but she was right. My daughter was with my mom, and I was stuck with her and them. Once again, I didn't say a word. I was getting good at it, not saying one word. That didn't mean it didn't hurt.

Over the next few months, Richard started really conferring with me about things. I don't know why. It was maybe because I could be trusted with it. One thing he had disclosed to me was the disappointment he had in Denise. It was then that he told me she had OD'd over three times. She almost died, and he'd had to pull guns and get her things back from three-card Mollie bandits. (It's a con game where they use three cards to trick you.)

He said he was through. He had really run out of patience with it all. I never told her what he said. I never told him about her extra-curricular relationships and the drugs I saw her do. I don't know if I didn't tell out of loyalty, if I was just good at keeping secrets, or if I just thought saying anything just wouldn't do any good for either of them. I figured he had to have heard about Indian Tony—her side-piece. I was sure she knew that anyone would get tired of picking you up from the hospital post overdosing.

For sure, she knew about him messing with his daughter. Didn't she know? Did he know?

Well, one evening, some of the secrets was disclosed because we came in from work and were in Yakima, and Denise went up to Richard's room. She and I had one room in the same hotel while he was upstairs. I guess that was so either Denise or I could have privacy with him. Well, she caught him in bed with Indian Tony's daughter. I don't know all that happened up there. I stayed in our room. She came busting into the room, telling me about how she'd caught them together, and she went after them.

Unsuccessfully, Sherri made it out of the room though. Denise began telling me how she was leaving him. That's when I got the whole story of Sherri and how this cheating had been going on. She warned me to watch out for her and told me to cook his eggs with cheese and to take care of him. She then was gone just like she came.

I was thinking, *Oh, great!* Now where does that leave me? I could have left too, but I didn't. I can't tell you why.

Sherri, what can I say about Sherri? She was a mess. She was full-blood Native American, definitely on the thick side, slick out the mouth, conniving, and a liar. Oh, yeah, I forgot—and spoiled rotten. She was her father's only daughter. Indian Tony, her father, as I stated before, was one of the largest dope dealers in the town and greatly respected for many reasons. Not too many people gave him trouble. She knew how to play her father like a violin and pretty much had her way and nearly everything she wanted. If anyone gave her trouble, even if she was wrong, her daddy usually took care of it.

I never saw, for the life of me, what Richard saw in her, and I still can't figure it out to this day. I just know he seemed to be crazy for her.

This time, he gave up his wife and his moneymaker. Denise was one of the best thieves on the streets. I hadn't perfected that skill yet; it was coming, but I made maybe $100–150 nightly whereas she was taking in thousands sometimes a night. Was he crazy?

I waited for him to come to the room and tell me his side. Of course, he didn't, but he informed me that it was now him, Sherri, and I.

Sherri didn't come with us home, but the next day, against Richard's wishes, Denise came by and took Suzette and some of her things. I was worried, and I know he was too. We were worried about where they'd be living. Denise really never had taken care of Suzette. All I could think was, *Poor Suzette.* Denise was overly high on heroin when she came to get her.

For the next few weeks, I worked hard. Denise had carried a lot of the financial burden. Sherri showed up, and he put us to work together in Downtown Seattle. The first trick we caught that she solicited was the police. We both went to jail. Richard bailed both of us out. I woke up the next day, and she had left me asleep in jail and told him they couldn't wake me. I knew then she was not to be trusted, just like Denise said.

Richard flew us both out of town together to Arizona.

The first tricks we caught there were the police. Talk about a piece of bad luck!

This time, Richard only bailed me out. I then was to go to work and bail her out. She didn't think I'd come back for her, and all the girls in jail told her I wouldn't, but I did. Now do I think she would have come and gotten me? Absolutely not. She was selfish and spoiled, and it was all about her.

We got out of jail and went to work but sent no money home. We had hooked up with Reggie. You remember Reggie? Reggie was the motorcycle gang member who went with Denise's friend. He was no longer with her.

Reggie showed us the time of our lives, escorting Sherri and me from club to club, each of us in opposite arms. He showed us a good time for about a week. We never phoned home (there were no cell phones) or anything. I wanted to on a couple of occasions, but my better judgment (my youth and having fun) told me not to, and I didn't. After about a week somehow, Sherri got us caught up with some not-so-nice guys. Not just caught up, but she actually had chosen one of the guys, which meant she was now working for this guy.

He was not a nice guy, and he demanded I strip down to nothing in a room full of guys. I was scared. I did what they told me to do. They wanted us to get into some bikinis.

I did. Once I obeyed, for some reason, they told me to get dressed and let me go. Sherri stayed with the guy she'd chosen, and I left and went to work. I never saw her again. I was glad because that girl was trouble. How was I going to explain things to Richard about her missing? I didn't. I made money for a ticket back to my mom's.

I thought I was hiding out. I wasn't. A few days later, Sherri showed up at my mom's house. I thought it was Richard. I was scared to death, but it was his younger brother driving. She asked me if I wanted to ride with her over to a dope house. She used hard stuff. I was still on pills. I needed some after that scare. So I jumped in, and we went over to a drug house off of Cherry Street. I really wanted to know how she had gone from choosing the man in Phoenix, Arizona, to beating me back to Seattle.

Obviously, she had been back to the house. Alvin, Richard's brother, had his car, so she definitely had been home. I should have known that it was a setup the entire time, but I didn't. Let me tell you what happened next. Alvin dropped us off, and Sherri did and copped whatever she had come for. I don't remember if I just waited on her or what, but when it was time to go, the car showed back up. I thought it was Alvin. It was not Alvin, and Richard had swapped places. He had put on the same hat Alvin had on. From the window, it looked like it was Alvin. As she and I approached the car, he jumped out. I didn't give him a chance to say anything. I just took off running as fast as I could. Now mind you, he was very angry.

Sherri and I had run off weeks ago. He was furious. I wasn't sticking around. He didn't look like he was in the mood to talk. I put my past track-and-field experience to work. I mean, I ran like crazy. He, with his sickle cell history, could have never caught me, so he jumped in the car and tried to catch me, but I weaved in and out of houses and cars. I saw flashes of that gold car, but that was all. I'd been set up by that Sherri. Boy, was I angry. I made it back to the house. They had lured me out of. Whew, I was glad to be back home in the safety of my mom's house. I had barely escaped what could have been a very ugly experience.

I lay low at my mom's for a while. I was glad to be home and spend time with my daughter. I didn't hear from Richard. I didn't want to either. I really thought I'd seen the last of him. Let Denise and Sherri deal with that maniac. Now I did have to go back to court for the case I had gotten a month earlier with Sherri, and I would go. Richard had bailed me out.

Back then, guys would leave their house papers or jewelry at the bondsmen so that anytime one of the girls or themselves went to jail, the collateral was always there, and you'd only be responsible for the 10 percent of the bond. It made it easy for everyone. The guys or girls could call. This means that as long as you had fifty dollars on you when you went to jail, they'd automatically come to get you out for a five-hundred-dollar bond. No one had to leave home. Just a phone call. Pretty smart. Everyone stayed out of jail for long.

After about a week, I decided to take a trip back to the streets of Downtown Seattle. I needed money. I made some and tried to try my luck and hopped on a bus to Yakima. Of course, I ran into Sherri who informed me she didn't know Richard was in the car, and she tried to convince me that Alvin had tricked the both of us.

I believed half of it because I know Richard would never, never allow her to go to the dope house. The story of how she got back from Phoenix and the whole gamut on her was a cause for suspicion.

She said she had to run back from the other guy, that I believed, but she was still under my suspicion radar for sure. (I had taken what Denise said at heart about watching her.) So far, she had been right. Sherri was definitely sneaky and trouble.

CHAPTER 24

Sherri informed me that Denise, of course, had come back home (she knew of nothing else) and because she and Denise could not reside in the same dwelling, she had left. They could not stand each other. Denise, I guess, had given Richard an ultimatum. Sherri must go! She did, and she was back now among her daddy's grace. During that few days, I started bleeding very heavily. I can remember actually having to use two to three pads and finally going to a small hand towel.

One evening Sherri and I were about to enter a dwelling together. It was in the afternoon, and Richard pulled up on us from out of nowhere and surprised us both. Denise was in the passenger's seat. He told me to get in, and I could see on his face he was serious. She stepped out, and I reluctantly got into the back seat. (It was a two-door Eldorado.) I had not seen her since the incident with Sherri (when she caught them sleeping together). I had not seen him since the chase in Seattle. My mind was racing.

I was stuck in the back seat with two very angry people who, right now, didn't care too much for me. I was seventeen. I'd never been in a position like that ever. No one was speaking, and we had a three-and-a-half-hour drive through many mountains and woods. I just knew they were going to kill me and throw me off of one of the many bridges we had crossed. On top of all that, I was bleeding profusely on a pad while traveling. What a nightmare. I had seen the beatings he had given Denise. I just prayed.

About an hour into the ride, he started telling me that I had run off and was trying to jump bail, and now that I wasn't with him any longer, he was taking a chance with his property. She jumped in and started calling me a runoff and telling me how I'd left her husband to fend for himself. Imagine that!

When I didn't respond, I guess they both got angrier. He actually told her to hit me. She reached back to do so, and I caught her hand and wouldn't let go.

If I was going to die, I decided I wouldn't go down without a fight. He told me to let her go, and I did. She turned back around in that car. She mumbled something smart, and then it was quiet again. I think I saw a little smile on his face. (The smile like this girl has a little heart in her.) He was right. I came from a long line of fighters.

Two and a half hours later, I was glad and relieved when he pulled up in front of the courthouse. I'd survived. Thank you, God!

He got out of the car first, and then Denise let me out of the back with a scowl. She didn't touch me though. Richard and I proceeded into the courthouse where he was to turn me in for his bond. As we went up the elevator, I was so disgusted with him and the entire situation. I had never missed a court date, and he knew that.

This entire show was for and about Denise and proving something to her. I said nothing to him; he said nothing to me. I was glad I did not feel like arguing, and I didn't feel good physically. I had been bleeding very heavily for days and had a small towel as a pad on at the time. I just wanted to get somewhere and lie down. I was weak physically and had been through a traumatic experience over a three-and-a-half-hour drive. I had no idea what they both had planned for me.

Many young girls had been killed for leaving their pimps. My cousin had been one of them. The authorities had found her chopped up in a gunny sack in Leschi Park months earlier. I was just thankful I'd made it in one piece back to Seattle. Even if that meant going back to jail, at least I was safe from the craziness of those Nobles.

As we walked into the courtroom, Richard talked to someone as I sat. I don't know what he said to the court clerk, and there was no one else in the courtroom. Then he abruptly left—without a word. As I sat there, flashbacks of the last few months and where my life had taken me crossed my mind. How had my life come to this? I sat quietly waiting to be placed back under arrest and sent back to the slammer.

I waited about an hour, and no one came. Finally, someone came and told me I could leave. I didn't understand, and I didn't care. I just got out of there and went home to my mom's—again.

Apparently, he hadn't revoked the bond. It was all a big scare tactic, and as I said earlier, it was a big show for his wife. She wanted something done about me because I kept running off. Never mind. She was the biggest liar and cheater ever. I'd never told a thing about her, but she grew to despise me the more he liked me.

Looking back, I guess it was understandable. She knew that emotionally she was being replaced by me. A big gap had grown between them. I know now long before I came along. She knew it, and I believe she knew it would never be fixed. They both, at separate times, had told me and shown me that in their own ways.

As I think back now, they were both very lost people, searching for fulfillment in a life incapable of giving them one thing close to it. Sad.

I made it back to my mom's again and got to spend some time with my daughter. She was much better, and I got to be a teenager for a while again.

I started going to Seward Park and the park down the street with my daughter. I was still occasionally working, but mainly I was just back to some normalcy. I was going to nightclubs again and just enjoying life. All the while, Richard was bringing me flowers and cards—without Denise's knowledge, of course, trying to convince me to come back. I really thought I had feelings for him, but I wasn't willing to deal with all that drama over his house.

Once, I ran into him in the club, and afterward, we just sat in the car in front talking. We always got along better when I left him. She and a few friends walked by and saw us. She was livid. He rolled the window down and asked if she was finished working.

She yelled, "I am now," and then pulled the door open. I just moved over. I didn't get out. She told him, "I see you have your habit with you." *Now I'm a habit?*

I had him take me around the corner to where my family I'd come with were waiting. She let me out, and that was the last I saw her. My friend Jennifer and I hooked up again. We were out, and I just lived life with some joy. It was nice to be free.

A few months later, as Jennifer and I were walking up Rainier Avenue in Seattle toward the pool hall, we were just talking about how we both despised Denise, and that's when it happened—a bad dream all over again. George Noble, Richard's brother, and his henchmen rode up to where Jeanne and I were and told me to get in the car. It was not a suggestion but an order. When I asked him what was going on, he then told me that Denise was dead and that they had found her outside, stripped of her fox coat and jewelry and left to die.

Jeanne and I both gasped because we both had been talking bad about her. I understood she was dead but wondered what it had to do with me. I hadn't been with Richard for about three months. I learned quickly what they wanted.

George stated that Denise was now gone. That meant that, as number two, I had to step up to the plate. Obviously, I had no choice in the matter. Gip, one of his henchmen, grabbed me, put me in the car, and whisked me away down the road back to Dawson Street, back to that house, back to Richard.

When they brought me to the door, Richard was standing there, looking like he was about to faint. I was thinking, *What can I do? Why am I here? I can't replace Denise.* I didn't know what to do. So I gave him a hug and tried to console him. They had been together for seven years and had a baby even if the love was gone. I knew she'd be missed by him. I know it all sounds awkward, me consoling him about another woman, but that was my life.

He began telling me the story of what happened. How they'd set her out on the street from the dope house. She'd once again OD'd for her final time. I wasn't surprised at the cause of her demise. I wasn't particularly happy about the way they set her outside and took her coat, jewelry, and money. He then began telling me how they had to go with guns and get her properties from those who had robbed her. It was all so sad. She was only twenty, and what about Suzette, her two-year-old daughter? She now would not have a mother. I wanted to go home. It was all too much. He asked me to spend the night, and I did. He just looked so bad. I cared more than I knew about him.

In the morning, I woke up to yelling and screaming. It was Denise's mother, Barbara. She'd come by the house to see Richard and Suzzette probably to emotionally support them both, and who did she find? Me. She was almost hysterical when she walked into her daughter's bedroom and saw me. I can't blame her. I know I would have felt the same way. All I could hear was her shout, "My daughter's not cold or buried yet, and you have another woman in her bed." She obviously hadn't been told by her daughter about our previous living arrangements or had no knowledge about me. Period.

I felt so ashamed and so small at that moment. I asked myself, *How do I keep getting into these predicaments?* It was very awkward. Barbara actually ran toward me with tears in her eyes. Richard had to block her from whatever she planned to do to me. He took a few hits and some very harsh words from her, and I went back into the room.

Richard came into the room with a look of exhaustion and hurt. I understood both of their feelings. He'd lost a wife, and she'd lost a daughter—someone they both loved. I was the one she wanted to take it out on, and I was the one he wanted to console him.

Somehow, we got through the next few days. Richard did all the funeral planning down to what she wore. I had no say so in any of it. Thank goodness for that! Kim, my friend, and I attended the funeral together. It was sad. A lot of people showed up—some were to look, some because they really cared, and some just out of respect for the game. It was expected.

I remember crying a lot. It was mostly out of knowing she was so young to die and partly because there were times when we got along when we were away from Richard. I also thought Suzette would now be motherless. Lastly, I knew I had some big shoes to fit in. She was experienced at what she did. I knew it would now fall on me. It was expected. I was number two, and now by death, I was moved up to number one. Even though we were not together, per se, when she passed, I stepped up.

CHAPTER 25

Within months, he was calling me his soldier. I held it down. I mostly worked in Yakima for the first few months, and then he had me back in Seattle. That's when Kim and I really teamed up and started making lots of money. It was around that time that we started dabbling with the hard stuff, heroin. Kim and I would split a twenty-dollar bag nightly. Richard really didn't care for her, but we made lots of money together, so he didn't stop me from teaming up with her. As long as we pulled the money in, he was quiet about his dislike for her.

During the next month, Richard had a woman here and there to work for him. That would usually be the time I'd run and take a break for a week or so. During one of those breaks, Eric had gotten out of prison, and we tried to get back together, but Richard threatened him. Eric had left for prison, leaving me a virgin and a schoolgirl.

He couldn't believe what he had come out to. I now was a full-fledged prostitute and was using drugs—drugs he had been using for years—but had never told me.

Our little rendezvous lasted about two days until Richard had gotten wind of it, and then that ended. Another time, I met a nice guy named Paul, and we talked for a few days. I had lost contact with Kim, not knowing that she was no longer with Tommy but with Paul. I guess he must have mentioned me to her. She told him of our history when she was with Tommy. At that time, Richard and I were in one of our many breakups.

When Kim figured I was thinking about being with Paul, she and I teamed back up, and off we went back to work from Portland to Alaska—in a cast, I had broken my leg by a fall.

Paul was really just for protection. We never even kissed. He basically was my shield and cover for the streets. I don't know why Richard never bothered him. Kim and I actually had a lot of fun in Alaska. I'd been there before, and things hadn't changed much. Paul himself was quite a hustler, so we all did pretty good. We all got along fine. I'm sure it was because Paul never touched me, so Kim had no reason to be threatened. I liked him, but my feelings still leaned (I know it sounds crazy) toward Richard. We left Alaska, and by the time I made it back to Seattle and to the cast doctor, the cast had had it. It truly just fell off right when I put my leg up on the table. Amazing! The doctor examined it and let me go—bare legged—with his blessing. I left him just shaking his head. I was moving so quickly. I was young, lively, and foolish.

Paul, Kim, and I left Seattle and headed south toward Portland where we stayed for a few days. We moved on from there back to Seattle. Kim and I were using every night—unbeknownst to Paul, of course. One evening, we used, and Kim always threw up immediately after fixing. (That should have been a sign it was a problem), and this particular evening, Paul caught her throwing up and put two and two together. They started arguing and fighting. I said nothing. He told me to go into one of the bedrooms and wait on him. I assumed he was going to give me the same treatment, so I was plotting a getaway while they were still fighting. Their apartment was on the ground floor, and the window of the bedroom I was in was right in front of the walkway next to the entrance door. I didn't know if I could pull it off or not, but I slid through that window and jumped onto the walkway. I landed like a cat on my feet and ran like a deer.

I knew that the after-hours club Richard was always at was a couple of blocks down the street. I kept running until I reached the after-hours club. I then caught my breath, straightened my clothes, and knocked. When I entered, the place was full. I saw Richard immediately, and he saw me. He pulled me into a corner, and we talked for a few minutes. I told him I had run and left Paul. I still had the money we'd made that evening. I gave it to him, and we left and went back to his house. Odd as it seemed, but I was glad to be back at the house on Dawson Street. We had sex, woke up, and went on as if I'd never left. I guess he informed Paul of my return because Kim started coming back to the house, picking me up for work.

There were no hard feelings between Paul and me. I guess because we both knew it was more like a contract of safety than a relationship. About a week after, I'd gotten back to the house. Richard woke me up and told me to get dressed and that we'd be going downtown. At that time, I thought we were going shopping. Most of the stores at the time were in Downtown Seattle. Malls were not that popular at that time.

I dressed quickly. I really enjoyed spending quality time with him. He could be fun at times, and he always had a great sense of humor. We got in the car and headed to Downtown Seattle. To my amazement, we parked pretty close to the downtown courthouses and jail. I finally asked why we'd stopped there instead of uptown. That's when he told me had been (*chippying*) cheating with a young girl. I knew her because she would babysit Suzette for us occasionally. He stated she had burned him (gave him an STD), and we were both there to get it taken care of. I was speechless. He'd always been a cheater. He'd cheated on Denise with me, but STD? We both ended up getting shots of antibiotics with the biggest needle I'd ever seen before. He did apologize, and I accepted. I figured at least he was man enough to tell me and fix the problem.

Kelly would no longer be the babysitter though. We agreed on that. We left the public safety building and headed uptown. We did do a little shopping. Well, he did. He always still picked out all my clothing down to my underwear. I'd gotten used to it, and he actually had excellent taste. After leaving Jay Jacob, one of his favorite ladies' stores, he took me to get ice cream. He was really trying to chummy me up.

We'd both forgotten to read the warnings of the medication that prohibited us from intaking milk products. I ended up really sick and in bed for the rest of the day. What a day!

I was back and forth to Yakima and then home for a few days. That was my schedule. Kim was pregnant, but she worked the entire time and used also. She ended up having the babies (they were twins) early. I remember they were so tiny they fit in a shoe box. Paul was a very good involved father. Unfortunately, only one of the babies made it, and one died. It was so sad. They had a small funeral because she lived some days. We were right back at it within days—working and using.

I lost a lot of weight, and my mother was worried, as well as Richard. I remember trying to confess to him I now was actively using daily and had been for over a year. His response was interesting. It was as if he did not want to believe it. I think he just didn't want to accept it. I was at a very low point in my life. Looking back, I can say that was one of my first times being depressed. I just kept on working. So many times, I thought, *How did I get to this point, and how do I get out?* But I'd get right back up and do the same thing. there was a point when I just started planning my funeral. All of it—music, scripture, and who would speak. I saw no way out.

Even though I was at a very devastating time in my life, I really did nothing to change it. I felt there was truly no way out at times. I remember feeling that way one day, and my girlfriend Vivette came by to visit me out of nowhere. I hadn't seen her in a while. She truly was light and a ray of sunshine. I didn't tell her, but she really made my day.

Richard and I were on and off. He had several different girls, nothing really permanent. I'd leave a few days or a week, and I'd be back. I'd gotten used to him and the chaos.

His friend Skippy and his woman had moved into the small room. That alleviated some of the tension. It gave Richard someone to talk to and me too. It had really gotten to the point where I didn't see him much even though I lived there.

I'd met one of his lady friends named Pam who had her own place. She allowed me to come there after work. I'd fix there and chill. Most days, I wouldn't get home until the wee hours of the morning. By the time I'd get in, he'd be getting up to feed Suzzette and take care of her. When I would get up, Kim would be by around three. We'd go out and about with the kids sometimes. She had a daughter, two years older than Tayona.

Paul kept her little one, and she had a live-in nanny named Barbara Ann. Most times when we didn't have the kids, we'd be shopping for that evening's attire. We would be buying new wigs and clothes. She'd taught me how to stash money inside the wig heads. Up until then, I had been pretty much giving Richard all my money. He took care of everything—bills, food, clothing. I learned quickly from Kim to always hold back. It was good, though, because I was able to do more for Tayona.

Richard never did take much responsibility for her. I assume it was because I didn't, or I didn't make him. I just felt like she was in a better place being with my mom. I saw a lot of things that weren't kosher for a young child. Suzette saw way too much even though she was young. I didn't want my daughter in the middle of that madness. There were way too many people, adults, in and out of that house. They openly drank and snorted both cocaine and heroin, and at some point, Richard was selling it too.

There was a time when what Denise said came to pass, and Indian Sherri came back on the scene and moved into the house. Richard and I weren't on the best of terms already. Her being in the house really didn't help. I kept myself busy outside of the house mostly, and finally one day, it came to a head. Her mouth got her and caught up with some of Richard's other girls, and they stabbed her. I was there at her house to join in. I just slapped her a couple of times. She ran to Richard, and because of her "dad," he hid me out in a motel for a few days, but I saw her dad at my sister's. He knew her boyfriend, and he knew me through Denise.

He wasn't angry at all and actually said he knew his daughter and the trouble she stirred up. He basically said he didn't like what happened to her, but he understood. She had a smart mouth on her. A few weeks later after she healed, she went to Yakima and came back with quite a bit of money, nearly five thousand, I heard. Kim and I had gotten some money also but not nearly that much, but he acted really funny with me. He always did around Sherri even though he would never admit it.

Anyway, Kim and I decided we would go to Phoenix for a week or so. Paul said he'd keep the baby. I brought Tayona over to keep Suzette company for a few days. I thought it would be okay because Cha Cha and Skippy were still there, and she and I were cool. I knew she'd look out for my daughter, which she did. The first couple of days were fine. Kim and I had a blast while we made money. It was winter, but it was 70° or warmer, which was great. I'd call and check in with Richard, and everything seemed to be fine.

Around the fourth day, I called, and Cha Cha told me it was snowing. I called and asked Richard to get both the girls some boots and coats. At that time, they didn't have winter gear. He said no problem he would. Two days later, they still had no coats and boots. So I called him. I found out through Cha Cha that when I mentioned it, he said something to me that hurt me deeply and changed our relationship instantly. He said to me, "I said I'd do it, but Tayona is really not my responsibility." I couldn't believe it. After all I'd done for his daughter, he would say something like that to me.

I had a feeling Sherri was near, and he was just showing off for her, but I did not care. I knew deep down in my heart he felt that way because he never really talked to my child. To have the audacity to say it to me was another thing. I was a thousand miles from home, and she was left in his care, and he felt like that. I just hung up the phone and went into the closet and cried my eyes out. I cried for everything I'd done for him and what I'd given up—two years with my child and a life a teenager should have lived. I cried a river.

Everyone has a breaking point, and that was mine, my daughter. Kim finally coaxed me out of the closet, and we went and got high. She was having some relationship problems with Paul too. That evening, Cha Cha called. She told me that Sherri had been locking the girls up in the room when Richard would leave.

I was livid. I left her in his care, not Sherri's. I caught the next thing smoking out of Phoenix the next day to retrieve my child. I didn't know how Richard was going to act when I got there, so I had my cousin Bobby, who was a good solid 220 pounds (Richard was tall but very thin), come with me to get my daughter and all my belongings. When I got there, I didn't say a word. Bobby and

I walked in. I got my daughter and my belongings, said my thanks and goodbyes to Cha Cha and Skippy, and left. I never went back to Richard.

Getting over Richard in the days and months to follow was not easy. Even though it had been a very volatile relationship, it was a relationship, and one of my firsts besides Eric. I had formed a bond with his daughter, family members, and friends, some of which I had grown fond of. Suzette really hadn't had anyone but me as a mother figure for two years since her mom passed. I felt guilty leaving her, especially knowing Sherri despised her because of Denise.

His mom and sisters had always been kind to me. Several Sundays when I wasn't working, I'd go to church, and we went to the same church. Tine, his mom, knew my family well, and I respected her a lot even though I wondered how she had produced such characters for sons sometimes. Phyllis, the sister closest to Richard, visited frequently, and I got to know her fairly well. His other family members got to know me well also.

It took a while to implant the thought of leaving permanently, but I knew it was for the best. I somehow could take all he dished out to me over the four years, but including my daughter, I just couldn't take. I felt like If you really cared about me, you'd care about my daughter. I don't believe he knew how to care. Pimping is a life where you really have to put emotions on hold. It was just part of the game.

I cried a lot for the first few weeks. I can remember being in Downtown Seattle in one of the big shopping stores. Fredrick and Nelson, it was called. It was a huge ladies' room with chairs and perfume dispensers, mostly Chanel 5. I was sitting in one of the chairs, crying, and an old woman came up to me and asked me why I was crying. I told her I'd broken up with my boyfriend, and even though I knew it was the right thing to do, I was sad about it. She grabbed my face gently and looked into my eyes and told me that even though I felt like dying, no one ever died from a broken heart and that it would hurt deeply for a while. She said that one day, I'd wake up, and a whole day would have gone by, and I wouldn't think of him. Then after a week, a month, and a year, she said, eventually time would get me over him.

At that time, with me being so young and this really being my first relationship, it didn't feel like it, but she gave me hope. I dried my eyes, gave her a hug, and continued shopping.

CHAPTER 26

My daughter and I moved in with my sister, her boyfriend, and my niece. The kids were three years apart and got along well. It worked out pretty good. I was still going out working so I was able to help financially with food and overhead.

It was nice being able to be a real mother. I'd missed a lot I worked mostly at night, so I got to spend time with Tayona during the day.

My sister was renting a house from our stepfather at that time. I thought it was a little strange because he attempted to molest her too. They had somehow managed to have worked it out. I had not seen him since the divorce. One day, he came by to fix something at the house. As he was walking up, I was walking down the walkway. (She lived on a hill!) I spoke and said, "Hi, Daddy!" (the only thing I'd ever know him as) without expecting anything but a hi in return. I got the unexpected. He turned around and looked at me straight-faced and stated, "I'm not your daddy," and turned back toward the house and continued walking.

I cannot tell you how badly that hurt me. It was mostly because it was unexpected. Another is that I had never known him to be anything else. It was like a brick had hit me in my heart. I cried all the way to the bus stop. I never said a word to anyone about it for years. It hurt too deeply. That day, I didn't come back. I just went and made money and got high. That was becoming my way of dealing with everything. It seemed to work at that time. So why not? I stayed high for the next few days. It really did ease the pain.

Over the next month and a half or so, I went to work and spent time with Yona. At that time, my sister had a live-in boyfriend named Edward. He and I got along fine. He worked construction during the week. On weekends, he worked in the clubs as a DJ. My sister did not know it, but he also used the hard stuff heroin. That's probably another reason we got along. I never told her. I knew she'd eventually figure it out, which she did much later.

Edward hung out with a guy named Billy, and he introduced him to me. Now Billy had a white woman who was a dancer (stripper). He worked at a bank. I guess you could have considered him a square really who was tinkering with the game. Ironically, he and this woman lived together and had a small child. (Sounds familiar?) We hit it off really good. I was much deeper into the game. I worked uptown, downtown, and out of town. He was really used to a pretty normal life. He worked during the day. His woman worked evenings in the strip clubs. He kept the baby while she worked. She was home to take care of her while he worked. With my schedule undetermined, it took a toll on his little happy family. He ended up moving out and getting his own apartment. He also ended up picking up a couple of more girls, mostly dancers and a few who worked the streets.

Richard did try to intimidate him at one point. He was smart enough to not bite. At that time, Richard was so caught up with Sherri. He really couldn't be a threat. She and he ended up getting married. She went to the penitentiary twice while pregnant. He ended up raising the children alone while she did time during both trips.

I really don't remember why Billy and I broke up, but we didn't make it long. We lasted maybe six months. He eventually went back to his little home.

Our relationship had created problems with my sister and Edward. I guess she figured what had been true that Edward had introduced me (just part of the game). My sister, Edward, and Billy and his woman before me used to all go out and hang out together. So you can see that it definitely caused some division between them all.

I moved on without problems. I took my daughter back to my mom's, and she and I made our home back there. By this time, my mom had moved to west Seattle in High Point housing. When I moved back, I ran into Eric Barnett again. He was living with a woman a few blocks away. He'd stop by occasionally. I still had that first-love feeling every time I saw him, but he stayed in and out of jail and the penitentiary I just couldn't get with it. Once again, I was free and by myself. I took that opportunity to go back and get my GED.

I enrolled in South Seattle Community College. It didn't take me long, and I had completed all five tests. I was really proud of myself. After all, I never went back to school for my junior or senior year. It had been almost four years.

I had a sugar daddy I'd met two years previously. His name was Tom. He helped me get my first apartment. I was so happy. For the first time, Tayona and I would have our own place. It went well for a while. Tom would come over every evening. He was a great cook. We didn't have any furniture, but we were happy.

Joanne, one of the ladies I knew, had a daughter, and she was getting put out of her apartment. She had a lot of furnishing and everything but beds, so I let her move in with me. It went pretty well at first. She wasn't very tidy, but I was, so I did the cleaning while she did the cooking. She had her own group of girls who she worked with, and I was still working with Kim at night and Vivette, Sharon and Jeanne during the day.

None of the girls got along too well with Kim, so that created some division. I did have Billy over a few times, but we never got back together. A few months after having the apartment, I got word from someone that Eric had gotten married. I couldn't believe it. We'd always said that if we did get married, it would be to each other. I felt so betrayed. I'd seen him and knew he was living with a lady. He'd always say it was a place to stay. I believed him because he always came around to mom's house.

One day, he had come by with a child on his shoulders and said it was his. I knew it wasn't. We laughed about it. He left, and I hadn't really seen him since then. I could not believe he married her. I cried all night. When I woke up the next day, I went right down to the King County Jail to go see what it was all about. I took my seat behind the glass window and waited for the guards to bring him. I was infuriated. It had gone from hurt to anger.

As soon as he saw me, he looked relieved and started smiling. I didn't see anything to smile about. I had come strickly to find out about the rumor of him doing a jailhouse wedding. He sat down, and I started pounding on the glass, screaming at him through the phone about the rumor. I reminded him loudly of our promise to each other to keep marriage vows sacred only for us. We'd made the pack when I was only fifteen. I was nineteen then, almost twenty.

He tried to calm me, to no avail. I got it all out then asked him to explain. He began telling me that they were trying to give him some time. She had several kids, five I believe. He said he married her to make it look good in front of the judge. He, her, and their family of five small children. He'd written the judge and told him that they needed him. It worked. They decreased his time after the jailhouse wedding and gave him a work release. He told me that he would be finished with that time in a few weeks. I was slightly skeptical, but it made sense. I guess it's what I wanted to hear. He told me he loved me and always would. He said the marriage was for convenience purposes only. He then began to tell me about the Whopper. He began asking me if I remembered one time when he, his best friend and his lady, and I had been with them when they sold some stolen goods about a year previously.

I remembered immediately because I wouldn't go to the place with him. The two of us, ladies, stayed in the car down the block. I'd run into him while I was out and about. He told me of these supposed-to-be Mafia guys who were buying up all his stolen goods. That's what he did steal.

He said they were taking everything, which seemed odd to me, but I was just riding. He and his friend Ronnie brought stuff to them for several weeks each time coming back with crisp hundred-dollar bills. They said and thought they'd hit the jackpot with these guys. Now a year had passed, and he was sitting in jail for a misdemeanor reading the papers and watching the news. He came across an article about an FBI sting in Seattle. The sting consisted of them receiving stolen goods over a month. They had set up this small warehouse to receive them in. They had pictures and names of all involved.

He held the article up to the window with fright in his eyes. He asked me what I thought. I told him it was probably them. He then began telling me that he had a plan to stay a step ahead of the Feds (ha ha). He was going to act like he was going to work like he'd been doing daily but just not return. He said the only reason they hadn't arrested him was that they wanted him to finish his time at the county. He was sure that once they released him, the Feds would be right there to pick him up from the jail. I listened. That's when I told him I had moved out of mom's house into my own apartment.

Very few people knew where I lived. Together, we came up with a plan that on Monday morning, he would go to work from jail and not return. He would come to the apartment. We figured we'd hide him there and get him a fresh identity. Back then, you could get birth certificates easily. We'd get him on a plane and down to Vegas where his good friend was living and where my god sister also lived with her pimp, Will, who was also related to Eric. We had it all figured out. Monday came, and they released him from jail to work. He worked to throw them off. After work, instead of returning to jail, he came to my apartment. I was glad to see him. We made love all night. I loved Eric, and he loved me. We were going to have a wonderful life in Vegas. *We'll start all over,* I thought, *and do it right.*

Joanne wasn't that happy with the arrangement; there was only one bedroom. I'd taken Tayona to my mom's that weekend. We got two mattresses. Alecia and Joanne were on one, and Eric and I on the other on the floor, but I was so happy. I was really looking forward to a future with him. Of course, that didn't happen. The first few days went well. I was able to get him a new identity. Then I started working on getting him out of the state. Eric could not hold his liquor well, and he continued to drink heavily. He made his way daily to the corner tavern near his mom's house. I stayed frustrated because I couldn't understand why he would drink and get into altercations, knowing the consequences he would face if caught by the police.

Nevertheless, he continued to drink. I myself now was not only using heroin but also had got introduced to cocaine. Belushi is what they called it—heroin and cocaine. It was named after John Belushi who had overdosed on the combination. Crazy that everyone knew he died, yet his concoction became famous after he died from it. We were a mess. I was getting high, and he was getting drunk. Both of us were being irresponsible. I was constantly trying to get him to leave.

Christmas came after a few weeks of him being out, and I had gotten my family their gifts. I worked hard to get his family some gifts also. When I purchased them all, I went to his mom's to drop them off, and surprisingly, Eric's jailhouse wife and her kids were at the house. I was surprised because I wasn't aware that his mom even knew about it, let alone knew her comfortable enough to have her overnight with her kids. I found out differently. I knocked on the door, and his mom stepped out onto the porch, which was odd, especially because I had an armful of wrapped gifts.

She explained to me that she felt really bad for the way Eric had done the lady, and to smooth his behavior out, she had invited her and the kids over for Christmas Eve (that day) and for the following day (Christmas). I was so hurt. I kind of understood, but his mom and I always had a very special relationship. I somewhat felt betrayed. I didn't say anything.

She continued to say that because she had invited them. It would be rude to have me enter the house. Just about that time, his wife came flying to the door, screaming at me. I can't remember all that she said because, at around the same time, Eric came. I was supposed to meet him there. I don't believe he knew about his mom's Christmas guests. Up to then, he had not seen her since he'd come straight to my apartment from jail. She began yelling at him to choose either her or me. He told her no problem and that the choice would always be me.

She just cried and yelled some more. His mom asked us to leave, and we did. She yelled obscenities at us all the way down the street. We spent Christmas with my family. New Year's Eve came, and Eric was still in Seattle running around.

We somehow ended up at the club on Jackson Street, nicknamed the Bucket of Blood. So many people had gotten stabbed and shot there. We happened to be around that location near midnight.

That's where we spent our New Year's Eve. I was very unhappy with it. I believed at that time that how you started your year would play out and affect your entire year. He was drunk again.

We started arguing in front of the club. Now my uncle, my mom's oldest brother, used to hang out there too. He saw us arguing and quickly came in between us. He said he wasn't having it, and he put me in a cab and sent me home. He sent Eric walking up Jackson Street. I went home. Eric didn't come home that night. He came home in the morning, and he had some money. I never asked him where he got it from. I learned later that he went to his wife's house and had her sell everything. He told her he was leaving and made her believe her and the kids were going with him, only for him to bring me the money.

I had no knowledge of his scheme. I had no knowledge that he had been with her. He never said a word. I learned this later from his daughter many years later. She dislikes me to this day because she believes I knew. I would never put children in a predicament like that. I, one day, want to apologize to her for not recognizing their marriage though.

Eric and I put that money with the money I made the next day and got him (finally) a ticket to Las Vegas. When I finally got him on the plane, I was relieved. I just knew he was not going to get caught and thrown back in jail. He made it safely to his friend's house, and I worked on getting my ticket and getting things settled at the apartment. I talked to Joanne, and she agreed to keep the apartment. I got Yona once again and settled her back at my mom's, and I hopped a plane down to Vegas to join my love, Eric.

On the plane ride, I kept envisioning this perfect life for us together, moving away from everyone and getting a fresh start. I really had big dreams for us. Once I arrived, I was so glad to see him. We made passionate love all night. This was a great start.

I woke up to screaming, yelling, and knocking on the walls. I jumped up, and so did Eric. Eric's friend was beating his girlfriend. I was shocked. He kept hitting her. Eric finally stepped in but not before her son was able to come out of his room and see the damage. Eric took him outside and got him cooled down. While they were outside, I was able to talk to his girl. She began telling me the story of how he'd gotten started on this new drug called Sherm. It was the More cigarettes dipped in embalming fluid. It was very potent, and you could smell it throughout the house.

She continued disclosing how this physical abuse happens almost daily. He'd get paranoid and extremely mean. She was so sweet and worked so hard to no avail. She felt like she was stuck because they now had a son. She worked every day, and he stayed home and got high.

It didn't take long for Eric to join in. That was one of the worst drugs ever. One night, they both got stuck out in the mud running from a force that was not there. They both came home covered in mud up to their waists. That's when I begin planning an exit from that house.

My god sister and Eric's nephew had been a couple for about a year, and they lived close to the Las Vegas strip we were living on the west side. I gave her a call and asked if we could stay for a few days until I could get money to get us to Phoenix, Arizona, which was our destination, to begin with. They both agreed that we could come, so we packed our things and caught a cab out of the west side and away from that crazy house. I felt really sorry for Jessie's girlfriend and the son. I thought it was so awful for the boy to have to see his father beat his mother constantly.

My hands were tied. She wasn't going to leave him. That was obvious. I couldn't do anything but move on, and that's what Eric and I did.

CHAPTER 27

The next week actually was a lot of fun. I had never been to Las Vegas. The strip was really exciting. The nightlife was twenty-four hours a day, and there was always something to do. My sister, a friend, and I got to see Sugar Ray Leonard at the Caesars Palace. It was the most beautiful hotel I'd ever been in. The rooms were huge, and the bathroom tub and bed were circular. Everything was done in gold and gold leaf. It was a truly amazing hotel and casino.

Mostly, we were in the hotels working. Sometimes we had to hit the street. It was no joke. The police there did not play. They'd threatened to drop you off in the desert. They kept the streets pretty clean from walking prostitutes. It was legal in some parts of Vegas, but you had to have a card and go through some red tape. I learned quickly to avoid the two worst officers. I'd just go inside on their shift. As I said, you could work any time of the day there because businesses were open 24-7. I'd often work on days. Sheryl, another friend of ours, had gotten with Paul (sweet), Kim's old man.

She and he lived right below Sharon and Will. I worked with her sometimes. One night, we hit a lick, and it was quite a bit of traveler checks. Paul and Eric got into a little bit about the split, but we all made a fair share of money, so it worked out.

Will, my sister's guy, never wanted her to split the money down the middle. That was the law on the streets that if we worked together and dated together, whatever we stole, we split it down the middle. One night, we came in, and I heard him beating on her about splitting the money. He was asking her how we had the same amount of money. It became a problem because I wasn't going to put her in the predicament to get beat up daily. I wasn't changing the rules; it was fifty-fifty or nothing. I talked to Eric about it, and we decided it was a good time to move on to Phoenix, Arizona. We purchased tickets over the next few days and flew to Arizona.

Eric had never been there, but I had on several occasions. I pretty much knew the town or, should I say, the area where the red-light district was. I found out much later that my knowledge of most cities was very limited to those areas.

We found a nice little cottage motel that had a kitchen, living room, and a separate bedroom.

It was located right on the strip, and it worked out fine. I could basically walk out the door, and I'd be on the Van Buren strip. We got along really well. It was really the first time since we met that we lived together. It had always been a few weeks here and a few weeks there because of his many trips to jail and prison. It started off fun. We got to actually get to know each other's likes and dislikes.

We would play dominos and watch TV during the day. It was nice. I hooked up with one of his female friends Tina. She was a twin. They were both from Seattle too. We did pretty good together financially, but she and her ole man had twin boys who stayed with them. They kept them pretty busy during the day. They also had a very violent relationship.

I never did get used to or like all the fighting. It seemed they did. I was told that many of the girls provoked a fight for the make-out that came afterward. I didn't understand it. I've seen it a lot though and heard it a lot. That was not the case with me. Richard and I had had numerous fights. I certainly did not want to be touched following a battle. I'm just saying. Tina also was into women. She would bring home a woman for her and Johnny to both have. She'd approach them as if she was getting them for him. They'd find themselves in quite a pickle once they joined what they called family and stable sisters. That's what girls were called when all were with the same guy.

Our time together didn't last long. She was much older and into much more than me though we did drugs in common. She even acted a little weird with that.

I met a six feet three inches tall young lady. She stood a foot above all of us, but she was really kind. She didn't have a man at that time. She got along well with Eric and me. She used also. She would come to our place to fix with us, and then we'd work. We worked well together also.

One day, I went out during the day, which was unusual, but we must have needed money or something. I caught a case. I thought he was a trick, but he was the police, and I went to jail. I was able to call the room and talk to Eric. I asked him to bring me a few dollars so I could have a commissary (toiletries, cigarettes, food, candy). I went to court, and the judge had given me ten days. I agreed to do the ten days even though I really didn't want to. I knew it would save money we really didn't have for the bond. This way, I'd be finished completely with the case. I wouldn't have to come back to court.

I didn't hear from Eric, or he never visited the entire time. I was so devastated and angry. I met a nice woman in there who had no problem sharing her weekly commissary with me. We quickly became jail friends. They had just built a new jail. Thank goodness. Everything was new in it. It had a lot of windows, clean floors, and beds.

For the days I was there, I worked in the laundry, so it made the time go by quickly. The day I was released, I didn't even try to contact Eric. I went straight to work and met a lady. We worked together for the next few days. She wasn't really my type. She was a little rough. I choose to be more of a pickpocketer. It took finesse, believe it or not. I found out pretty quickly that she was a snatch grabber. She had a car though, and she used heroin also.

I made it work with her. I stayed the next two or three days with her. She had an apartment of her own.

One night, we worked the dirty movies. We would act like we were going in to see the movie together. We'd knock on individual doors asking if they were interested in dating. We did pretty good. When we'd get or steal extra money, we'd meet at the car. So we had a getaway. Before, we'd have to run and hide or wait in a cab. That's when I found out that having your own car made a big difference. We also got to work in different towns on the outskirts of Phoenix.

She opened my eyes to broaden my places of work.

One night, we went to cop some dope, and we ran into Eric. Now I hadn't seen him since I'd gotten out of jail. I didn't wish to see him either. I really felt like he had abandoned me. He could have left money even if he didn't visit. She and I walked in, and I acted as if I didn't see him at all. I felt like he was able to buy dope. He could have at least come to see me. He had a new identity and social security ID. It was what I'd gotten him. He was now Terry, not Eric.

I wasn't for all those excuses. Instead of me being angry and being the one to tell him off, he flipped it on me and gave me his famous what-about-me-struggling-out-here-without-you act. I told him I had nothing to say to him and went to walk behind my friend who had already copped what we came to get. The next thing I know, he had snatched me from behind and pushed me into a bedroom. He slapped me and pushed me into the small closet door.

Now Eric and I had argued, but he had never—in his life—put his hands on me before. I was surprised. I just started screaming as if he was killing me. He just looked at me as I picked myself up. Everyone in the dope house ran in there, thinking he was beating me to death. When they ran in, I ran out and jumped in the car with my friend. That was the last time I saw Eric for seven years. That night, I stayed with a friend. I just stayed high over the next twenty-four hours, crying again and knowing it was over. I wasn't going to be with anyone who left me in jail.

Richard or Billy had never, and I wasn't going to stand for it. I made up my mind to go back to Seattle and try to start over. Hopefully, my apartment was still waiting on me. Over the next few days, I called home. Joanne let the apartment go. Tom, my sugar daddy, was acting funny. I didn't know, but he had found someone else to take care of. He did agree to buy me a ticket home and left it at the airport for me. He informed me that he wouldn't be there to pick me up. I left for Phoenix with Eric, and he found out.

The day before I was leaving to go back to Seattle, she and I went to cop some dope. Now I had never really used more than a twenty-dollar bag of dope. I had just really gotten up to that. So what made me think that I could do an entire fifty-dollar bag? I don't know. That's what this girl did every time. She was a serious user though. Kim and I split a twenty-dollar bag for the last three years. I was way out of my league with her. She had a habit I was just using to ease the pain and feel good. She needed it. That evening, without thinking, I agreed to do a fifty too.

I was hurting knowing once again Eric and I were over. Tom had left no apartment. Poor me. Poor me syndrome. I did the whole fifty even though she tried to talk me out of it. I woke up in the freezing cold alley at 100° weather, soaking wet but alive. I overdosed five times in my life. This was the first. I was so scared but so thankful she stayed with me and worked on me until I came to. She definitely knew what to do to revive me. She iced me.

She put something dry around me, walked me to the car, and took me back to the apartment. I couldn't remember a thing. It was just as if I had gone to sleep and woken up. The next day, I jumped on a plane and headed back to Seattle. I arrived safely—alive. Thank God. When I returned to Seattle, I was briefly happy. I didn't have my apartment any longer. I was staying with my mom and daughter in High Point projects now. At first, I missed Eric a lot, and though we did not speak, I thought several times in my mind about going back to him. I didn't.

I continued to work the streets at night, but I did get to spend a lot more time with my daughter. She was around five and was going to begin kindergarten. I met another guy (or sugar daddy) who kept me with money and all the alcohol my family, friends, and I could drink. He was a gambler, and I later found out he dabbled in drug dealing as well. For the most part over the next year and a half after returning from Phoenix, I remained single and stayed in Seattle pretty close to home, which was unusual for me.

My mother hooked up with an old boyfriend who was now in prison. One of her associates also had a boyfriend in prison. They both teamed up and became traveling buddies to Walla Walla Prison. I didn't really like the idea of my mother having a relationship with a convict whether she'd known him or not, but I really could not convince her of the inevitable. She pretty much had her mind made up. She was in love again. He proposed to her some forty years previously so the story went.

CHAPTER 28

Something happened, and she ended up throwing the engagement ring into the creek. They hadn't seen each other or had any contact since. I knew within my gut that it would come to a tragic end, but she was set on making it work. I say that because first, he was still incarcerated, and I know about the jailhouse romances and how they say just what you want to hear while they're inside. Once they got released, it would be a whole other ball game, and amnesia would show up.

Second, he had requested something my mother never did— which was to be dishonest. He told her a sob story and confided that he was in need of some cash to pay a debt. A debt? In jail? Really?

Anyway, to my surprise, she came completely out of her character and complied with his wishes. The problem wasn't the money. It was only twenty dollars. The problem was that he wanted her to illegally transport the money inside the prison through one of her effaces. If you know what I mean. That was a sure telltale sign that this guy wasn't on the up and up. I couldn't talk her out of it, but I was carefully assessing the situation. He was scheduled to be released soon.

Before I knew it, he, Tony Cabigas, was released from prison, and he and my darling innocent mom were planning an extravagant wedding. On the day I met him, I knew he was on drugs. I was on them myself, so I knew right away.

At that time, they were distributing methadone to drug addicts by the hundreds, and he was a recipient as well. I didn't want to rain on my mother's parade, so I didn't pursue the negative feat I knew was coming. I took part in the wedding. It was huge. My sisters, a few of my mom's friends, and I were all adorned in beautiful pink hats and dresses as we paraded down the aisle as her bridesmaids. She looked beautiful. She had the wedding of her dreams witnessed by over three hundred people. Lights, camera, and action. She was so happy, and he nodded and scratched (telltale sign of being high) through the entire ceremony.

For the first months, I stayed close to home. Tony was really nice to me, my daughter, and my mom. He was working at the ship-yard but, directly after work, he'd go downtown or uptown and get extra stuff to get high. I knew this because Seattle is a small place, and we ran into each other copping drugs on a few occasions. I never brought it back up to my mother. I knew that eventually, it would come to light.

The funny thing was that we actually ended up becoming very close, even to the point where I ended up calling him dad. My daughter called him grandpa right away. They had a great bond. He had a great personality, a tiger growl, with absolutely nothing behind it. His smile was so bright and could melt the room. He was paid a hefty settlement, and he bought my mother everything she desired. He really treated her well.

The house really was run like a well-oiled machine. He picked up where I'd leave off with my daughter. He came home before my mother from work. He'd pick my daughter up from the girl's club and get dinner ready for the both of them.

I appreciated it because most times, I was up and gone in the streets to do my thing, prostituting to feed my habits primarily. I was still using heroin, but I had now added cocaine to the equation, and that called for more money because more was being spent. Adding cocaine put my addiction up to a whole different level.

With the heroin, I was spending somewhere along the lines of twenty to forty dollars maximum daily. The cocaine took up to hundreds of dollars daily. I would meet up daily with my good friend on Yesler street about one o'clock in the afternoon. That would just be the start. We would prostitute, using intermittently until around nine or ten. When night fell, my downtown shift would start, and that would pay to supply the cocaine habit to the wee early morning. Sometimes it would be daylight. I'd just be getting home geeked out of my mind on cocaine and broke—only to wake up and do it all over again. It was truly a vicious cycle. It was one I was unable to stop for years.

That became my life. I would get up to go to work (the streets), buy drugs, and go up and down all night long. I would make it to the school and to different activities my daughter was involved with, but for the most part, that was my daily regimen. The state was paying my mother benefits to take care of my child, and sadly, I was living right under the same roof.

Because of addiction, I was incapable of doing it myself. Nothing came before the drugs. I would have never admitted that then even though the facts pointed clearly to that. I forgot to mention that my two sisters and my younger cousin were living at home as well, watching me run in and out of the house. I'd pay them to iron my clothes and do the cleaning and other things around the house. What a terrible example I was setting. Unfortunately, my younger sister and my younger cousin followed in my footsteps into the life of prostitution eventually. It didn't go well for them either. I am only thankful they did not pick up the addiction I suffered from as well.

Back to my story. For the next two years, most of my life was a big drug blur. I chased the drugs constantly. I was in and out of my mom's house. Then my stepfather Tony introduced me to one of his friends. He was a hard worker but a stone cold-alcoholic, who also tampered with drugs occasionally. He was crazy about me the instant he saw and met me. He worked with my stepdad Tony (by now, Tony and I were best buds and were both using). At the shipyard he'd been working for over twenty-five years, he had never missed a day's work. He probably would have been a great companion, but he had some of the same issues as me. He lived in an apartment near Downtown Seattle, and I spent a lot of evenings there. I never moved in, but I was there in the evenings when I wasn't on the streets.

He supplied me with lots of dope or money, so I oftentimes didn't have to hit the streets. I have never, to this day, seen anyone drink quite like him though, and that always stayed a deterrent to any real relationship forming. So he remained a sugar daddy, just another chess piece in my game. You could say we used each other. He was getting what he wanted—sex, and I was getting what I needed—money, drugs, and some security financially.

About a year after meeting him, my god sister and I decided to take a trip to Yakima to try to stack some money. Now she had just had a baby. The baby was just a few months old. Our great minds got together and took the baby with us on our excursion. Not too smart. The second evening out, we both caught a robbery case. Her bright self, in the middle of a cash transaction involving money exchange, decided to pull a knife out and strongly arm rob a small-built Hispanic man who could not speak English at all. Probably he was later found out to be illegally working here in the fields.

He was scared for his life, and he jumped out and through the front window of the motel. He somehow got away and called the police. Now I was just as surprised as him at my sister's action. Neither he nor I saw it coming. I was so mad at her. Our room was just a few doors up, and I just went to bed because I had a bad toothache. Anyway, I had been to the doctor the day before, and he prescribed a pain med. I took two frustrated (we still didn't have money, and he had only given us twenty dollars apiece before he took his leap) and climbed in the bed. My night was over.

I closed my eyes with major regrets about taking this trip with my sister. She left in a cab to go pick the baby up from the babysitter. The Hills family were permanent residents and had agreed to babysit the baby while we worked that evening. A short while later, I woke up to a loud knock on the door. It was my sister and several police officers. I was told to get dressed. My sister and I were shuffled into a car and taken downtown Yakima, and I guess the trick must have been in a car and pointed us out as the culprits who attempted to rob him earlier.

The rest was the beginning of my worst dream.

The story goes that the police had been looking for two black girls who had attempted to rob—but in his words *robbed*—a man and had been asking all cabs and drivers if they had picked anyone up that fit the description. Well, the cab driver who drove us to drop the baby off earlier that evening remembered us and thought we fit the description. The police were waiting for my sister and staked outside of the Hills house. She brought them to me for what she was told for questioning. Not so. They locked us up, and three days later, they charged us with first-degree armed robbery. I was devastated. They had split us up. They kept her in isolation. Luckily, I was able to stay in the population. I have claustrophobia. For three days, I slept. I managed to bring my prescribed pain pills.

Back in those days, they administered your prescriptions without question, so I received Tylenol/codeine three times a day.

They kept me under. I really believed I was going to wake up like I had so many times with the guards saying, "Roll 'em up," "The charges had been dropped," or "None had been charged." In those days, they could hold you without charging you for up to three days. So foolishly, I wasn't too worried. I'd spoken to the detectives. I thought it was back to the streets as usual. It didn't happen. We were both charged and given court appointments at our arraignment. Our court dates were set on the same day at about one hundred days out.

I was devastated and scared. We were facing up to ten years in prison for over forty dollars. The trick told them it was over two hundred dollars, which was not true. The baby had to be rescued by my cousin who had no kids of her own. She also worked at the shipyard, had a stable job, and was willing. Thank goodness for family. At least, the baby was good.

I couldn't believe the mess I was in. Both our bonds were set at ten thousand dollars. No one had that kind of money. My friend or sugar daddy remained faithful. He made the three-and-a-half-hour drive up to visit me every Saturday. He'd leave fifty dollars each week. It was enough to buy a commissary for both my sister and me thankfully. Up until then, I had never done more than thirty days in jail, and with ten years hanging over my head, I was scared, angry, and not pleasant to be around.

I was stuck in a five-by-five cell with one bunk bed, toilet, and sink nightly. I was freed during the day in a small dayroom with about twenty other women. During the first two months, I played cards, talked stuff, cussed, and fussed. In the third month, a great thing happened to me. I met an older white lady who was jailed for a minor traffic violation. She was very vulnerable because of her age, color, and charge. See, there were women in for murder and much more serious charges.

They despised those who had a few days because some would never see daylight again.

She was somehow placed in the cell with me, and I befriended her. That gave her protection. In return, she got three days to witness the gospel of Jesus Christ to me. It was music to my ears. See, I had known him since I was young and had had great experiences with him as a child. During my early teens, I searched for him, but my mom stopped going to church, and I started running with the wrong crowd.

For three days, she and I had Bible study. When she was released, she left with a promise to come back with friends and visit me, which she kept. I took visits and money from my sugar daddy, but I looked forward to her visits. She and her friends took turns every weekend, making visits and sharing the gospel.

We didn't see our court-appointed attorney until two weeks prior to the trial. After talking to both of us, he put our case together and went to trial. It was a three-day process. We had a jury trial, so the first day was spent picking the jury and opening arguments on another day. On the third day, my sister and I took the stand in our defense. Then the victim with an interpreter took the stand on the last day. Each day we return back to the jail, our attorney seemed encouraged. Even the escorting officers seemed convinced we had it in the bag. Closing arguments were completed, and then the waiting began.

My sister and her best friend attended court every day. Hours later when the jury came to a decision, we were called and shuffled back to the courtroom with great anticipation, just knowing we'd be going home soon. Everyone felt we had it. They asked us both to stand to receive the verdict. The head juror read the verdict—guilty of all charges. I could barely stand up. The rest was kind of a blur. I was handcuffed and brought back to the jail. I had no words. I said nothing. I just sat in my cell on the bed in shock.

I couldn't believe it—guilty. I'd gotten myself over my head this time. I was looking at doing ten years in prison. The rest of that day and evening in my lonely jail cell was horrific. I kept asking myself, *How did I get myself into the mess I am in?* And even better yet, How am I going to get myself out of it? So many times previously, I had been jailed and released. Thinking back, I really thought it wasn't going to happen to me. I had always gotten away with real robberies up to this point.

I truly believe my youth and ignorance had me believing I was somehow invincible. Not this time. I had always been told by the old-timers, "Don't do the crime if you can't do the time." I'd heard it a thousand times, but I never thought it would apply to me. Well, there I was, facing ten long years for twenty dollars and a charge of weaponry I never used on the victim. All that didn't matter. The verdict had come back quickly, and I had to deal with it.

The next few days were long and hard though my god sister didn't seem to be dealing with it as I was. Actually, she was playing cards and getting along as if nothing changed. I, on the other hand, was devastated. I thought of all my childhood dreams of being a teacher and a nurse. I thought about my daughter who was just only seven years old. She'd be seventeen before I'd be out to see her. I did a lot of self-examination over the few days after the verdict and while waiting for our sentencing date.

That weekend, one of the Christian visitors came to visit like they had been doing for weeks after the friend I'd protected had gotten out. Back in those days, your visitor would walk right up to a window after being ID'd and patted down. They would just call your name, and you would pick up the phone and talk for fifteen minutes. Well, on this day, she prayed with me first as they always did. Then she asked how things went in court. I do remember telling her that we had been found guilty of armed robbery and were facing ten years.

I don't remember anything more of that conversation. When I looked up, I was back in my cell on the bed. I was told by the rest of the bunch that I had fainted during the visit and had been carried back to my room. That was a first for me. I guess the stress from the court and the verdict had caught up with me. I was looked over by the nurse and staff. Once I was left alone in my cell, I rolled off the bed onto my knees and said the prayer of repentance and asked the God I hadn't talked to in quite some time to come into my heart and change it and to forgive me. I got no audible answer, but I did get great peace. I cried my eyes out. I slept like a baby.

When I woke up, I felt a change I had never felt—so free even though I was still behind bars. I don't remember the prayer the lady prayed over me at that visit, but I do know that it reached God who reached down and touched me on that day. I'll never forget it.

I began reading the Bible the friend had left me. I remember starting in the New Testament and reading the gospels over and over again. I did a two-and-a-half-week fast. I apologized to a lot of the girls to whom I said stuff and had hurt. God immediately took the cigarettes and cursing away. A lot of the girls and guards couldn't believe the change in me. I spent the next month waiting to be sentenced and studying the Bible.

My sister and I kind of grew apart at this time because I was no longer her card partner and running buddy. I spent most of my time in my bunk. I was only eating one meal, so they'd barely see me. I did continue to buy her a commissary weekly. She didn't have anyone to financially support her. My male friend continued to financially support me and visit me weekly. He, himself, couldn't believe the drastic change in me either. It was all God's doing though.

He was glad to not be getting cussed out each visit. It was the girls in jail who told me how badly I'd talked to and treated him before my conversion. I don't think I realized how bad my mouth was or how I treated others. I learned a lot about myself over those last thirty days.

One day, I was in my cell studying, and it came to me to write a letter to the judge who'd overseen our case. We had a jury trial, but the judge was the one who ultimately would be doing the sentencing. I did, and what I told him was the truth. I started out by stating that I knew the life I had been leading was incorrect, and I was working on correcting it. I also told him that I had committed a ton of crimes I knew I was guilty of, but I told him that this one, I did not commit it in the way it was presented, which was somewhat true. I hadn't been the one to pull the knife, and there was absolutely no two hundred dollars or more involved (which made it a felony). It was twenty, but I omitted that in the letter too. I pleaded with him to consider giving me another chance. I told him I felt like I had turned a new leaf and would prove it if given the opportunity. I sealed the letter, gave it to the court, and humbly waited on our sentencing date.

On the 101st day of our jail stay, we were marched back into court. My god sister and I sat beside our lawyers.

Our cases had been tried together, so that required sentencing together as well. I looked at the judge, but he wasn't easily read. My Christian buddies and family members and male friends were all seated behind there to hear our fate. I can truly say that was the scariest few minutes of my entire life. I know now that I had accepted Christ that either way it went, I had help from above. This means that if I got the ten years, I'd do it with God. That gave me quite a bit of peace, but I was still fearful of what the penitentiary held.

The judge spoke and said he'd received my letter. He'd taken it into account, and his decision was to not send us to the penitentiary but to place us on a ten-year probation, and he gave us credit for the time we served for 101 days of incarceration we'd done. I couldn't express the relief I felt. All fear melted, and I really felt God had intervened to give both my god sister and me a second chance.

The tears flowing this time were tears of joy. The walk back from the court to the jail felt like floating. God did it, and that evening, we were released from Yakima county jail. I vowed I'd never return back, and up to date, I have not. My male friend was there to take us and drove for three and a half hours back to Seattle. Not much was said in the car. I was just so thankful to God. I also thanked my friend for supporting me throughout the three-month stay in jail. He had not missed one weekend visiting me and financially supporting me and my god sister.

Both Sharon and I moved in with Mom. I was glad to be back home and to see and spend time with my daughter.

CHAPTER 29

I enrolled in school at Seattle Central Community College and found a church called Macedonia Miss Baptist after visiting several of them. I joined and became involved in serving there on the usher board. I got baptized and continued to enhance my relationship with God. I read the bible daily and really felt like I was getting closer to God. It had been a long time since I felt God's presence in my life.

Since I was a little girl, I had been searching for that feeling. My life seemed to be improving. I was doing well in school. I was getting to be a mother to my daughter once again, giving my mother the opportunity to just be a grandmother instead of having the responsibilities of both. Quarterly, I had to report to my probation officer. He'd always tell me how well I was doing. My grades were As and Bs. I rekindled my relationship with my friend Angela. She and I spent evenings together, taking turns cooking and watching the children.

Everything was going well for a while until I started feeling like I was missing something. That feeling came way before I acted on it. The only way I can describe it was discontentment and loneliness, even at school and church. I kept feeling like I was missing something. Sharon had moved out long ago and had gotten into trouble and got some of the time promised to us. I still occasionally saw Vivette, my friend, but I was still lonely. My male friend had found a new girl to take care of, and I was okay with that. He drank way too much anyway.

I started slacking off going to church, and I started dating a married guy whose wife was locked up in prison. The good thing was that I'd gotten off my probation with only two years in because of good behavior and good grades.

Once I met him, I was off and running back to my old ways. He and I moved into an apartment, and before long, I was right back to my antics. I started sneaking and using drugs again. I'd stay home and babysit the neighbors' kids during the day. Once 10:00 p.m. came, I was right back on the streets of Downtown Seattle, prostituting.

It didn't help that the boyfriend also used occasionally, so he had no problem with me using. Lots of times, I shared it with him. Most people at the time had no idea what my nightlife was.

I put on an excellent act. During the daylight hours, I seemed like the good-looking stay-at-home woman. I was living a double life. On the weekends, his son and my daughter would come and stay with us. His father and stepmom adored me. They felt like I had finally settled down with their son. Very untrue. James was a hard worker and did construction, but on Fridays, he drank like a fish. I never had problems with getting all of his checks to take care of the household, which I did by God's grace. Because I had started back using almost daily or every evening, I was a good partner, good parent and stepparent, and wonderful housekeeper. The problem with living a double life though is that will be exposed eventually. It took a while, but it did.

On the outside, it looked like James, the kids, and I were just one big happy family, but that was so far from the truth. There were some good times, but it came to a crashing end.

During my time with James, something very tragic happened. My niece who had been born perfectly fine had contracted meningitis when she was a month old. This left her with severe handicaps. She needed medicine and around-the-clock care. My younger sister had another daughter. The time I had spent at my mom's over the past three years before meeting James, I had made it my job to get her off the bus and play with her until my mom and sister picked her up. We'd gotten really close. Something happened that made my sister snap, and she'd given the kids away.

This had been devastating news to both families, her father's also. My mom had tried to retrieve the kids, but the process was ongoing, and in the interim, they were both in foster care. When I got the call that the oldest niece with handicaps had drowned in their care, it was one of the hardest days of my life. I'd just barely grasped the fact that my sister had snapped and given them away, but now my niece was dead. I was so angry, confused, and distraught. I don't think I've ever hurt like that before.

That day, I did talk to God. It was something I hadn't done in a while, and I asked him why. With the lifestyle I was living and the way I was carrying on, I wasn't sure he'd answer me, but he did. And he said that I shouldn't question him and that she belonged to him. God began to explain to me that it didn't matter how she died. I asked him why she had to die in such a way with strangers drowned in a bathtub away from everyone she knew and loved. God told me that it didn't matter how she'd died and that she was alive and with him now, laughing, running, and playing. He told me that she had no more pain and no medicine to take, and she was now whole in a new body, without any handicaps. God proceeded to tell me that I had no right to ask. He always knew what was best for all. I didn't challenge or argue with him. I apologized to the Father, but it did not stop the hurt.

The adopted family called and said they would be having a gravesite funeral only. I could not believe it. The service was held in a small town called Onalaska Washington about seventy miles southeast of Seattle. My family caravaned to the service. When we got there, I just remember seeing a big plot of grass and a few people standing way off. I couldn't believe it. They started the service without us. My sister was there, but it was evident that she had had a mental breakdown. I just remember seeing that little casket in that great big field, and the closer I got, I could see my darling little niece lying there with her favorite teddy bear on her side. There are no words to explain the hurt, pain, and anger I felt. Someone needed to be held responsible for leaving a multi-handicapped five-year-old who could not lift her own head alone in a bathtub. I felt nothing but hatred for the adopted family, and then they had the audacity to start the service knowing we were on our way. When I looked at my beautiful niece lying there in that casket, I also noticed that all her hair was cut off.

They'd cut her hair. She always had beautiful hair from the day she was born. Just anger and hurt were my feelings. As I was looking over her, I caught a glimpse of my younger niece who was running around. My sister had given her away also. All I could think was, *What is now going to happen to her?* If this terrible thing happened to Dálana, how could we be sure that Antionette, my young niece, was safe?

As her father approached me, we didn't even have to speak. We both looked at each other and looked at his younger daughter running freely and the one lying in the casket, and without saying anything, we'd nonverbally formulated a plan. I distracted everyone while the kid's dad got Antoinette into his car, and without notice, he and she were gone down the back roads of the countryside onto the interstate and out of town. When I was asked where she was, I said I knew nothing. In my mind, I thought that the safest place for her to be was with her father. My sister had snapped. These people were irresponsible, and my lips were sealed. I knew nothing about where or who took Antionette.

My niece's father contacted me a few weeks later and asked me to keep her. I agreed. At the time, I really thought I was doing the best thing for her. At least I thought she was with me safe and being loved. It never occurred to me that my sister, my niece's mother, had just lost a child and now didn't know where her living child was. Antionette stayed with us for about a month. Her dad helped her financially quite a bit. It was no problem for me. I was taking care of two other children whose moms worked during the day. They were all about the same age.

When her father picked her up at the end of the month and took her to California, I had no idea at the time that would be the last time I would see her for years. I just knew she'd be in good hands. I guess it did work out for a while with her dad and his girlfriend in California, but something happened. My sister got her back some way. This time, she made it permanent. She did an open adoption. My whole family, especially my mother, was devasted. Once she did that, it was all out of our hands.

Life for James, the kids, and me went pretty much the same for the next couple of years. He worked, and I'd babysit during the day, and we worked and drugged into the early mornings. It was only God that kept me from going way back out where I had been before being jailed. I say that because I was displaying the same behaviors. I hadn't really changed anything but my address.

James had asked me to marry him. He was a good guy, but we were really different and had different values. I think we stayed together as long as we did because of the kids. The kids were happy with us when they were there. Somewhere, James was introduced to crack, and I knew the path cocaine will take you down. I was using heroin and cocaine myself, but James was very influential. That was the difference between him and me. I used because I wanted to when I wanted to. I think he used more to fit in and because it was offered.

We slowly grew apart, and I think he saw it coming—a breakup. So he did what I'd asked him not to do again—propose. He waited until his birthday, which was December 25th after church on Christmas in church. We attended service with his parents. It was after church that he proposed—in front of his parents.

In the forte, he dropped to one knee, and came out of his pocket with a ring. He popped the will-you-marry-me question in front of everyone. I was so angry because I felt like he did it in that way to pressure me. I felt intimidated. I said no and ran to the car. I moved back in with my mother. I left the apartment and everything in it with him. I only saw James one time after that after about two months. He saw me walking. I believe he had been looking for me. He pulled up on me, hopped out, and asked me what I was going to do and whether I was coming back. I said no. I could see the hurt in his eyes, but I just knew it was over and that he was not the one for me. I was not going to put him or myself through anything else. It would have just prolonged the inevitable.

Once again, I was back at my mother's house. My stepfather and I had become great buddies by now. We were even sometimes exchanging drugs. It didn't take long for me to go right back to my old antics. I was no longer attending church. I was working the streets day and night again.

CHAPTER 30

While in passing, I ran into Vicki, Eric's sister, and we started boosting together. I'd walk in, take a coat off the rack, and walk outside, and she'd return it and vice versa. We did that throughout the Christmas season. It was Vicki who introduced me to some guys from Cali who sold dope. There were several of them, and they, such as "Tommy," all packed big guns.

Well, I found a great dope connection, I thought. I bought dope there for the next month or so on a daily basis. Even though I hated guns, it didn't stop me from copping. They had the best drugs in the area, and they always gave you a deal too.

Four guys ran the apartment. Three of them worked for the apartment owner, and one guy worked for himself. Later on, I found out they all came from the same set (gang) out of San Francisco, California, and were all childhood friends. I really think I became intrigued with the whole setup. It was run, for the most part, like a well-oiled machine. It was a business.

I'd been around dope houses for years, but none were run so systematically as this particular one. I'll explain. It went like this. You knocked, and they asked who it was. If they knew you, one person would let you in at gunpoint while the other three had guns pointed directly at you as well. You'd be asked what you needed. Money was taken by one of the three or the independent seller. Drugs were given, and you were turned back out the door. No one was allowed in who was not known or escorted by someone well-known. It was run for twenty-four hours, seven days a week. It was something else that was new. Most Seattleites shut down after two or three, and if you wanted the hard stuff, you'd have to wait until morning. But not this group.

They took the money all day and all night, and whatever you had, they fit the drug to the amount of money you had. Another thing that was different. I'd always get the two-for-thirty-five deal, one hard stuff and one coke. The independent dealer had taken an interest in me. Every day, he'd say something to show me he was interested, but I didn't bite. I kept it business. I never did credit or was short. I always got in and back out. It had been a few months since I had officially broken up with my boyfriend of three years. James. I didn't want to jump into anything yet. He did have beautiful brown eyes and dark chocolate skin. Another reason for showing a lack of interest was that I always told myself that I'd never get involved with a drug dealer. I always felt like if I did, I'd never get off drugs because they would always be available.

A couple of weeks later, while I was still running off and on with Vicki, shoplifting, and drugging, her brother Eric, the love of my life, showed back up. I hadn't seen him since I left him in Phoenix, Arizona. I had been told he met a Southern girl from Memphis and had been with her for the last past years. They had even moved his daughter down to stay with them. I heard it was pretty serious, and they tried to get married, but he never got divorced from his jailhouse wife because she was still angry he'd left her for me.

When I heard he couldn't marry her, I was relieved. He was the love of my life. At the time, in my mind, he was always going to be the one I would end up with. When we saw each other, I melted. It was like we'd never been apart. We spent the next few days together at Vicki's as usual. Her home had always been our meeting and loving place. We both copped together at the spot. He was quick to let all the guys there know that I was his longtime girlfriend and about all the history we had. We were inseparable for the next week or so. I was happy to have him back in my life again. We always had that passion for each other. I was definitely under the impression that we were back together, and we were both going to give it another chance.

Boy, was I wrong. One evening, I showed up to the drug spot to cop, and the private dealer began asking me about Eric. I thought it was odd because Eric and I had been together daily through the spot. His first question was, "Now how long have you, guys, been together?"

I answered him that I met him at fifteen, we'd broken up a few times, but I'd known him a good while. He then asked a more curious question. "Now are you, guys, together, and if so, why was he there the previous night trying to sell a ticket to Phoenix that his *woman*—his words—had sent him?" He began to proceed to tell me that Eric's woman in Phoenix had gotten a lot of money. She'd gotten a good sting (stolen money from a trick) of roughly around five thousand dollars. That was quite a bit of money back then. Still, she had asked him to return home. He'd agreed, and she'd sent him a ticket. He'd known this and had talked to her over the last few days. He never let on to me anything about it. Then the dealer who liked me anyway was elated to give me the news, stating that Eric left that morning with the ticket no one in the dope house would purchase and was now back in Arizona with his so-called X.

I was devastated. I didn't let it show. I got my drugs and left. I cried all night. He'd deserted me again. The awful thing was that he had not let on at all and had not said one thing about leaving. The next couple of days, I stayed upset, but I kept working and getting high. After about a week, I was able to face Vicki again, and she and I made some money and went by the dope spot. The independent dealer was there, and I don't know if they were in cahoots or not, but Vicki invited him over to her place, and we all drove out there. That was the first time I'd been introduced to a chocolate rock.

I don't know if I was just so hurt about Eric and was trying to hurt him, or if I was just acting on impulse, but I started a relationship with Tommy following that next day. Soon I was caught right up with a fast-moving drug dealer and his entire company. I remember one day running into James as I was walking down Yesler. (Tommy lived a block up the street.) I was surprised to see him.

I'd never known him to frequent that area. I realized afterward that he had come looking for me. He had such a sad look of desperation on his face. His question to me was, "Is it really over? Are you coming back?" My answer was an abrupt no! I'll never forget the sadness in his eyes. Sadly, I heard after that he really started into drugs heavily. He'd always *chippied* around with them. His true drug of choice was alcohol. That was the last time I saw James Beckworth ever.

Tommy

Tommy was a very interesting-looking and acting person. He was a dark chocolate man with very light eyes. I had always vowed I'd never be a drug dealer. Never say never. Our relationship started a little rocky because of the circumstances around Eric, but he was always a businessman and was the one and only of the crew who sold drugs for himself. All the rest worked with and for Diamond. Tommy copped from Diamond but was an independent worker.

Anything and everything that came through the house as far as clothing jewelry, furs, and merchandise, I got the first pick at it. Within a month, I had a wardrobe and jewelry on each hand, necklaces, watches, and furs. I really just had to be there with him. It was the first time I'd held a gun. He gave it to me and told me anytime someone knocked at the door, I was to point it directly at the door. Everyone else who sold out of the apartment such as Lucias, Red, and Diamond's brother-in-law had guns and did the same. It was an action they brought with them from California. They'd all been knowing one another for years. It took a bit of getting used to, but I caught on quickly. It was really for the safety of us all.

Tommy was a very gentle man and, most times, was very balanced. Whatever he had, he shared with me. He was also good to my daughter and family. He had a temper though, and when he got angry, he was violent. We had several episodes over the years. The five years I was with him were filled with drugs and the life that goes with it. It was during this time that I got my first habit. I was addicted to heroin badly. I had it every day, so I didn't really realize it until I went to jail one Friday and didn't get out until Monday. It was the worst time I'd gone through in my life. I could feel the sweats and the feeling of things crawling on me. I got no sleep. I was throwing up until there was only gall.

The amazing thing was that there was a woman who came to jail for a traffic ticket and had to stay the weekend also. I'll never forget her kindness. She kept wiping my face and taking the sheets off and on as I needed. I couldn't eat, but she made sure I was constantly hydrated with water. She stayed up with me the entire time. I know now that she was an angel sent by God. Without her, I might have not made it.

When I got out that Monday, I vowed I'd never get hooked on heroin again. I never did. I'd always put cocaine in with it to offset it. I never wanted to go through that again.

When I got out, Tommy had gotten a room downtown monthly. We moved from there to another hotel. That's where my daughter came to stay with us. He was really kind to her. I can remember one day when I sent her to school, and by ten, it was snowing nonstop. School had let out, and I was wondering how she'd get home. It had snowed nearly four inches (very unusual for Seattle). There had been no foreknowledge of the snow.

All the buses were at a standstill, and I was in a panic. She went to school near the Mount Baker area. She was in a private school, a Montessori. I'd made all the calls I could think of where she might have gone, but no one had seen her. It had been hours since school had let out. Just when I had put on clothing to go out and find her, little Tayona, at nine years old, was at the door. She walked miles in a snowstorm but made it home. When I asked her how she did it, she just followed the road up until she saw Downtown Seattle. She knew that's where we lived. She kept walking until she saw the Seattle Hotel in Downtown Seattle. That's when I knew my daughter would always be okay. She was a fighter then and still is.

When we left there, we moved in with my mom and stepdad for a while, but that didn't work that well. We eventually ended up moving to San Francisco, Tommy's hometown. That's when and where my life took a turn for the worst. Someone had always told me not to go to someone else's hometown. I found out why.

We lived like nomads from room to room and house to house. He knew everyone, and I knew no one. We used most of the drugs we obtained at night, having to start over every day. Tommy was the last born and was the only child left out of nine. All his brothers and sisters had died. His nieces, nephews, mother, and family seemed to cherish him. He was the only memory they had of their parent and, in his mother's case, children. It was a sad situation, but he played on it and got his way with almost all of them.

The violent episodes continued. The drugs ran our lives daily. I never felt so beat up mentally, spiritually, physically, and emotionally. By this time, I was back working the streets daily and nightly.

We were fighting constantly. I can remember feeling so low, wondering how I had gotten to where I was at.

As I was sitting one day on the stoop on the backstreets right off of Haight Street, I remember reflecting on my life for one of the first times in a while. Normally, I was so busy getting money, spending money, getting drugs, selling drugs, and using drugs. It's a vicious cycle. I never had time for reflection, but this day, I did for some reason. I asked myself, *Why am I living from post to post?* My mother had a warm house back home. It was freezing there.

I asked myself, *Why am I constantly fighting off these different women who continually chased Tommy when I don't really care that much about him? How can someone who had such a good start in life, who had been to college, and who had dreams end up on a corner far from home, doing the unthinkable?* Every car that I got in and out of just confirmed my agony. I remember thinking I'd call home and just talk to my daughter and mom. I thought that would get me out of my depression.

It did the opposite. When my mom answered, I could tell she was upset about something. It seemed my daughter had been maturing at a very rapid speed. Her size increased monthly. My mom knew heavy breasts ran in the family, but not at this rate. She was twelve and already in a triple-D cup. Because she didn't understand what was happening, she assumed that she was possibly pregnant. Pregnant! I didn't hear anything else after she said that. I just hung up the phone and nearly collapsed. When I got myself together for a few minutes, I remembered there was a small park nearby.

I walked there swiftly, sat on the bench, and cried for hours. I hadn't cried like that in years. Pregnant! I couldn't believe that my daughter, at thirteen, was pregnant. I was sixteen myself when I had her. It was the most devastating thing in my life—having to raise a child alone and being a child myself. It was the last thing in the world I wanted for her. There must be a mistake. It had to be. Thank God, it was. A few days later, she started her cycle, and we found out she was still a virgin.

I was so relieved. What she said to me on the phone that evening was so profound it was life changing for me. Out of the mouth of babes, she said to me, "Mommy, you've been in and out of town, in and out of my life. I've just rolled with your lifestyle, and I've never said a word about it to you. Mommy, I'm going through puberty, and my grandmother is not my mother. You're my mother, and I need you now. I need you to come home."

I cannot tell you how deeply that cut and affected me. I felt so low. It was true. I had been running in and out since she was six months old. I decided to leave her temporarily in the custody of my mom at six months old. Now she was a teenager and still in the care of my mother, not her mother as she had stated.

That was the second eye-opening moment just in one week's time. I headed back to the park for another good cry. The only difference was that, this time, the tears kept coming. I was still working the streets daily and nightly getting high, but nothing seemed to stop the tears in between. I was constantly in the park crying. Finally, I did something I hadn't done in years. I said a prayer in that park and asked God to get me home. I even checked the Greyhound to see the cost. It was seventy-five dollars. I said to myself, "That's reachable."

I met a guy that evening. He gave me more than enough money. By the next day, I spent the money on drugs and alcohol. Every twenty or fifty dollars that came into my hands went right back out. I felt so low. Never once could I have believed that I could not put together seventy-five dollars to get back to a child who needed me. I was worse off on drugs than I wanted to admit. I was back in the park daily. It was a good thing Tommy and I were on one of our breaks (we had many). The tears came back. He would not have understood. He was okay with his life. I was not. I knew that if I could get home, I'd be okay. I was going to try again to save.

I ran into Tommy. He and a friend were in a car when he rode up on me. I got in, and they went on with their conversation about the large amount of drugs they had copped. Most times, I would have been right at the moment with them, but I kept thinking of my daughter and what she said. As I was riding along in the back, music was playing. An old song came on by the Chi-Lites called "Have You Seen Her." I don't know why that song made me think of myself, but it did that day. *Where am I? Who am I?* All these questions came to my mind as we were riding along. That song had always brought me joy, but that day, it made me look at where I used to be in my teens—happy, joyous, and free compared to where my life was at that moment.

I yelled over the music for the driver to pull over and let me out. Neither Tommy nor the driver reacted at first. Then I screamed even louder. Tommy turned around and said, "You want out?"

I said, "Yes."

It was then that he told the driver to pull over. Tommy looked at me and showed me a bag of dope that was in his hand with a smile (an evil one). He said to me, "You will never leave, and we have all this dope." What an insult!

I told him, "Watch me!" I opened the door, hopped out, and began walking. They skirted off. I don't know how to describe it, but I felt free.

I endured five years of drug abuse, physical abuse, and emotional abuse that was supposed to be love but had no love in it. I had so many battle scars outwardly and inwardly. I had been stabbed in the leg by him and scarred on the face by a cake cutter. He broke my nose and busted my lips on several occasions. Then he'd feed me drugs to make up. I deserve so much better. I came from better. These were the things going through my mind as I was walking back to the park to cry another river.

As I was sitting on the steps on the backstreets, crying, a few days later broke with the clothes I had on my back, holding my head in my hands, I looked up, and there was a small, short woman in front of me. It was strange because I'd just put my head down, and there was no one at all on the street besides myself, but there she appeared out of nowhere. She lifted my head up by my chin and asked me why I was crying. I told her about the story of what my daughter said. Then I said in a whisper, "I just want to go home." She asked me what it would take to get me there.

I spoke up and told her I needed seventy-five dollars for a bus ticket. She reached into her pocketbook and handed me a twenty-dollar bill. She said that's all she had, and she wished me well and walked off. I remember looking down to retrieve my purse from the step to put the money in. When I looked up, she was gone. I hadn't even had a chance to say thank you. She seemed to disappear just like she had appeared. She had to have been an angel when I look back.

My goal for the day was fifty-five dollars to go with the twenty dollars and make seventy-five dollars, and then I could purchase a ticket home to Seattle. The money wasn't even in my hands fifteen minutes and I was off to the mission district to cop dope. I remember when I handed the dope dealer that twenty, something said to me, "See, you are hooked. You think you can do this, but you're hooked." I used the dope and was right back on a run. I broke the promise to the lady and God that I would not spend the money but save for a ticket. As I sat in the park that evening, it was my voice that told God I needed his help to get home. I couldn't do it on my own. I cried myself to sleep that night.

As I stepped out the next morning around ten o'clock, everything seemed as usual, but it would never be again. As I flagged a man down in hopes of breaking luck (getting a first date or trick), he pulled over. I was thankful because I was very hungry and hadn't eaten since the morning before.

As I got in, I asked him if he could take me to get something to eat. He agreed. I'd often use this tactic to have time to feel a John out and get a look into his wallet. It also would give me time to ensure he wasn't a police. As we were sitting in the restaurant, we had a great conversation while I filled the empty hole in my stomach. The conversation was very casual. As we were driving back to the street, I was planning on throwing in if he wanted a date. I decided to wait until he was just about to drop me off. That way, if he said no, I wouldn't have to walk back to the area.

As he pulled to the curb on the small hill where he had picked me up, I turned to ask him the question. Before I could get it out, he began talking. What came out of his mouth was something I was not prepared for, but I couldn't move. It was so prolific.

He turned to me in a gentle voice and said, "I know what you think I am, but I'm not a John." He began telling me how God had gotten him out of bed and told him to start driving. He told him that there was someone he wanted him to minister to, and he had sent him right to me. He then stated he was a street minister and also did prison and other outreach ministries. He told me that I had to be super special to God for him to wake him up so early and give him such specifics down to the location I was at. He then asked me if I knew the LORD Jesus Christ and if I had ever received him in my heart.

I started bawling and told him yes. I told him of my church experience as a kid and how I'd found him as an adult again in jail but had left him. I told him about the drugs and mishaps I'd been through since I had backslidden. I continued about the week of crying, the conversation I'd had with my daughter, and wanting and trying so hard to go home but was overtaken by drugs. Then I told him of the woman who I thought was an angel who'd given me twenty dollars. I completed the conversation by telling him how I prayed to God for help over my life and to get me home.

He listened intently, and when I finished, he showed me a beautiful smile and said that everything was going to be all right and that he was sent to see about me, and that's what he was going to do.

I exhaled and just fell back into the cushions of the car. I couldn't believe it. God had answered my prayer. I just needed to surrender! It was right there on the backstreets of San Francisco that he prayed the sinner's prayer with me. I felt so light, so free, so happy.

Then he did the unthinkable. As I was getting out of the car, he shuffled me back in and told me he did not want me out there with the wolves. He was taking me to his home. He did.

Eddie da Costa

His name was Eddie da Costa. He was truly sent by God. Eddie was truly a light in the darkness. Not only had he prayed with me, but he also took action and literally rescued me from the streets of San Francisco. Eddie and his sister shared a home that had been left to them both. She resided upstairs, and he lived in the basement. Eddie took a big risk by taking me in. One was that his sister never approved of me being there. The second was that he didn't know me and had just met me hours earlier before he basically snuck me into his basement residence.

Eddie was a nice-looking Hispanic man in his forties. He had a great smile. He was so knowledgeable about the Bible and had a great passion for it. The first thing he did was put a Bible in my hand. For the next few days, that's all we did—read and talked about the Bible. It was such a wonderful relief after the self-made hurricane I had put myself through for the past five years.

He fed me and taught me for about a week. Amazingly, I went through no withdrawals or cravings (besides ice cream). It truly was remarkable. A week later, he got me a ticket home. Just like that, I was restored to a sound mind, soul, and spirit and on my way home.

My mom and my daughter were both there at the Greyhound bus station to meet me. I hardly recognized my now-teenage daughter. She and I embraced and cried together. She was standing eye to eye with me. I'd been gone only a year.

It was really tough at first when I returned home. I was filled with a lot of guilt for having been an absent parent. My daughter was happy to have me with her daily, and it gave my mom a great break also. It wasn't long before I found a nice small church in the south side of Seattle. It was one I had been to years ago with my cousin.

One night, my cousin and I were out clubbing like we used to do regularly. After we left the small club, we walked across the street. We heard music coming out of the storefront church. I don't know why, to this day, because we, as I said, had just come out of the club.

We both had our shorts on. We both were drawn to the little church. As we entered from the street, we walked right down the aisle, and both gave our lives to Christ. At that time, we left tearful, but nothing changed in our lives. I always remember that night. So when I went searching for a church, now some fifteen years later, I chose this small storefront church to be my permanent church home.

There were just few members, and most of them were from the pastor's family. He preached an awesome sermon, and you could feel the Spirit of God in that place. I began bringing my daughter weekly, and I was gaining a lot of knowledge of the Bible. I was so excited again about how God had really changed my life that I told everyone I knew about it. Soon, I was bringing people in the neighborhood and loads of kids to the church. We were there all day on Sunday and deep into the evenings on Friday. So many of my friends and children gave their lives to the Lord at Faith Deliverance Church. It was a really special place.

Eddie continued to stay in touch with me, and every couple of weeks, he would send fifty dollars I can't tell you how much that helped and meant to me. We would talk weekly, and I'd report on what God was doing in my life. Everything was good. It was one of the best times in my life.

I thought about returning back to school, but one day when I was planning, I heard a voice say, "You're a nurse." It really surprised me because I'd always thought teaching was my journey. I never liked hospitals, nursing homes, or being around sick people, so I thought that was an odd statement. Not only did I think of it, but I also said out loud back to God, "I did not want to be a nurse."

For two weeks, I fought it and pouted. God can outwait anyone, and that's what he did with me. He just let me pout, kick, and scream for those two weeks. Then he gently just said it again, knowing that I wasn't going to win this one. I said to God, "I'm going to look for a job in the medical field." I found one for a certified nursing assistant in the West Seattle area where my mom lived. Even though I had no experience, they trained me on the job with pay.

I remember being so nervous during the interview. I hadn't worked in nearly twelve years. I had gotten that felony and had quite an extensive record. I'll never forget the interviewer looking at my application. I was hoping in a way that she'd turn me away. I really didn't like the idea of caring for sick old people, but she didn't. She smiled at me. Her name was Trish Leiman, and she said, "I'm going to give you a chance." She hired me that day.

I was actually a little stunned, but I told God I was going to do it his way, and I really wanted to please him. Within three months, I became an employee of the month, and I began to love caring for others. That was the beginning of my nursing career. Everything was great. I didn't make much money, but I was able to help my mom and buy a few things for my daughter.

Around six months after being home, I met a young lady up the street, and we quickly became friends. Her name was Angela Bradley. She had two kids at the time, and a couple of months later, she became pregnant with her third. We were very close, and I brought her to church with me, and we both were attending regularly. Her third child became my godson, and I adored him from birth. She allowed me to name him also. The next few years consisted of work and church. That was my life. It was truly fulfilling. Eddie and I always stayed in touch with each other.

The pastor had a daughter who, I found out, went to school with me in elementary. We were close in age, and Angela and I both befriended her easily. We'd oftentimes do extracurricular activities like movies, other churches' events, and things of that sort. We all became very close. One day, she approached me and stated she was attracted to me, I didn't know how to take it at first. *What does she mean?* This was the pastor's daughter, and she was the pianist, the choir director, and very involved in the church. She grew up in the church. I'd always admired her. It seemed, on the outside, that everything was great for her, but you have to know that the grass is not always greener on the other side. Things that appear to be one thing can fool you. She certainly did!

I really didn't know how to respond to her because I was shocked actually. Now I had some woman-to-woman experiences in the past, but I had always been paid to do these acts. I'd always been curious. Curiosity killed the cat. I should have remembered that. Within a week, we were involved in a forbidden relationship. I knew after a few weeks that this was something that was not going to have a good ending, but my curiosity got the best of me. Before I knew it, I was in the church in a relationship with the pastor's daughter.

I can't tell you how low I felt daily. I wanted out, but she was very persistent. It seemed like while I was looking for a way to stay in the church, she was looking for a way out. It was disastrous. I'd messed up again, and I felt so low. I started using drugs again and started drinking. She started using drugs also undercover.

It snowballed down. My friend started using too. Angela had two more kids by now. The last one was now my second godson, and I named him also. Angela knew something was going on even on the day she'd given birth. She'd said to me, "I know you and her are in a relationship." I denied it. I never admitted it, hoping I could end it and get back to God. It seemed the harder I tried to end it, the clingier she became.

Once, I even admitted to the pastor our disastrous doings and apologized. I really meant it. She had gotten so angry and called me a coward and a traitor. I just wanted to end it and get my beautiful life back. I knew the relationship was wrong and was dragging me back to my old ways. I gave in to her whelms. Somehow, I felt responsible for her. I don't know why. I do remember her father, my pastor, warning us. If we did not stop it, we would be turned over to ourselves.

I never forgot what he said. It happened just that way.

Adrienne

Adrienne and I moved into an apartment in Burien. We were both using constantly. I changed jobs to be nearer to work. I was working in a developmental disability clinic (DD clinic). I enjoyed it. I worked a lot of doubles. Adrienne was still in banking. Once again, I left my daughter with my mother, but after a year, my mom told me she was going to move up to the Cascade Mountains to take care of her mom and that I needed to come and get my daughter. She stated I had been in a stable place for over a year and that I was able to take care of her. She had a point. My daughter moved in, and shortly after, she realized the relationship we were in. It really hurt her, but she loved me so much that she went along. We moved into a two-bedroom apartment soon after. We seldom used at the house, but we would go to friends' places to use frequently.

I did not know much about the whole gay world, but I learned quickly. We had several friends in the gay community within a year. I was very surprised to find out that it had its own set of rules, areas, clubs, and ethics.

I constantly was looking for a way out of both the drugs and the life. I don't know how to explain it other than it was some of the worst times of my life. I wanted to get back to God. Occasionally, I would make it to some church, but I felt so distant from God. I tried everything to get off drugs and out of the relationship. It was so dark. I finally came up with the idea of going to school for nursing at the nudging of a male nurse coworker. He insisted that I would make a great nurse.

I took him up on it and moved to a ten-by-ten-mile island—very small. My oldest sister allowed us to stay with her until we got our own place. The boss who had given me my first job had moved to the island and was the head nurse. She told me I'd have a job waiting. I did. She hired me, and I began working and going to school at the satellite campus located on the island. Amazingly, I did very well. The move had cut down our using, but on weekdays and weekends, we were in the bars. When we could, we'd drive to the city and use. Thank goodness we never found a drug connection on the island. Oftentimes, we would go to Vancouver, BC, to party and use.

We did get our own place, and things didn't get any better. We were always arguing. I was always wanting out of the relationship, but she never would leave. I don't know why I felt so responsible for her, but I did. She hadn't worked in over two years. I was working, going to school, and trying to take care of her too.

Eventually, we moved to Mount Vernon where the main campus was. Things really got bad there. We found drug connections there. I don't know how I got through school. I was up all night using. Many days, I would come home, and the dope dealer would be in the apartment. They would be using in the early evening until dawn sometimes. I was still working at the nursing home and still going to school. It was a nightmare.

One good thing was that I found a small church that I attended frequently, but God was quiet. I longed so much to have that relationship back with him. I knew it was impossible to do if I stayed in that relationship. I just didn't know how to get out. I didn't want to hurt her. My daughter moved in with us for a while until she had her first child. It was nice having her and my first grandson there.

When she moved to Seattle, we were both using again. We never stopped; we just did it at others' houses. I do remember one day she walked in after we had used, and my daughter was so disappointed. She'd had her suspicions, but it was now confirmed. I'll never forget the look on her face. I was once again caught up in drugs.

I failed my final exam and had to wait for a year to go back into the program. Drugs and alcohol played a big part in it. I was getting very little sleep. I remember using that day feeling sorry for myself. That day, I OD'd again. No one was there. Adrienne was now working at a small coffee shop. I had injected drugs and woke up hours later. I know it was nothing, but God. I had a small mark on my forehead. That's the only way I knew what happened. God had spared my life once more.

I entered back into the program the following year, and I did it. I passed the final and graduated from nursing school with my RN. We were the first to take the board exam on the computer. I passed that with ease and obtained my RN license.

Once I graduated, we moved back to Seattle. We were using regularly. I got a job at a dialysis clinic, working daily and using in the evening. I finally got the strength to tell Adrienne that I wanted out of the relationship. I told her we were toxic. I told her I wanted a change. I wanted to get back on track. She took a bottle of pills and ended up in the emergency. It was there that I finally got help.

CHAPTER 31

The psychologist at the ER recommended that we separate. That was my way out. Finally, someone verbally told her that it was time to split—a professional. I told her in front of him that I agreed, and that's when the miracle happened. She moved out into her own apartment. I told her I'd move, but she stated she would. I let her take everything she wanted. She was gone in a few days. The first thing I did was fall to my knees and thank God. I repented for all the wrongdoings. I invited God back into my heart. I found a great church and began attending. It had been nine long years of separation from God. I was thrilled to be back in the arms of my savior.

I joined a wonderful church. It was one of the largest churches I'd ever joined, but the pastor was such a great teacher. He and his wife and two daughters were responsible for one of the fastest-growing churches in the city. I attended on Sundays and on Wednesday nights. I learned so much under him. I believe that's the first time I was taught by a preacher rather than being preached to. It was the first time I had ever asked the Holy Spirit to come into my heart. He did, and in the upper room, I called it. (It was the room upstairs where they did individual prayer.) I asked a woman to pray with me until I received the gift of tongues. She did, and I did. It was then that I knew I was complete. The next year, I just soaked up all of Tony Morriss's great teaching.

My life was great I was still working in dialysis, but they had given me a new position where I worked in the education department. I got a great increase in pay, and I now loved my job. I always loved teaching. My home was full of calmness, and I had a new grandson who I kept on the weekends. We did everything together. My daughter now had her own place. Life was wonderful.

I ran into an old friend who said she had seen Eric Barnett. She had run into Eric—the love of my life. At that time, he was still in a treatment center for drug abuse. That should have given me a clue. It didn't. I jumped right into a relationship with him within a few weeks. It was a big mistake, but I was in there, trying to save him as if I could. My friend Kim even made a statement about that. She said I was always trying to save people. I should have listened to her, but I didn't. I always told myself I wasn't a quitter. What I started, I should finish.

That statement is so untrue, but it's what I lived by at that time. I know now that you can get out and change your circumstances at any time, but back then that was my mission statement. There were problems from the very beginning. Eric still wanted what he wanted. Within a month, he managed to leave three different treatment centers. Each time, he swore he was being mistreated. I'd run and rescue him each time. He really didn't want treatment. He just wasn't ready, but I hung in there with him.

He finally got to the Salvation Army treatment, and he did very well. He was always a great manager, and he excelled very quickly. After he had been in the program and doing well for about eight months, he gave me a ring and proposed to me. I said yes, but I didn't want to get married right away. We never set a date. Things actually were pretty good. He didn't really like the church that I attended. I loved it and continued going faithfully.

He had church daily because he was in the Salvation Army, and church was mandatory. I was getting closer and closer to God under the leadership of a great pastor at my church. This was the church that I'd finally asked God to fill me with his Holy Spirit in the upper room with another seasoned saint. I believed and received it. Then one day in prayer, God spoke just like he did about the nursing. He told me I needed to go to Bible college. He was very clear about the name and state. I couldn't believe it. He wanted me to go to Texas. He was so specific. After what I had gone through with the whole nursing and how I didn't want to do it, I learned to be obedient. The reason I had even heard God's voice in prayer was that my pastor at that time challenged the entire congregation to ask God what our purpose was. I'll never forget that day.

It was so eye-opening. He guaranteed us that once we asked that question, we'd be answered by God. He was right. I got an immediate answer as to what my purpose was. I wrote it down in a journal, and I still have it to this day. It truly changed me. For so long, I'd just been existing. Yes, I was on the usher board and involved in the church, but I'd never in my life put that question before the LORD. He answered, and he said, "Your purpose is this. You are a missionary, healer, prophetess, intercessor of prayer, and a teacher."

I couldn't believe it. Once he listed those five things, a great peace and a new hope came over me. I looked each position up and found out that all five of those positions were something and areas that God was using me in already.

For the first time, I felt complete. That's when he told me I needed to go to school also. I did not fight it. I began making calls to Texas within the next few days. The first thing I did was call the school that he had given me—Bay Ridge Christian College. When the woman picked up the phone, I began to tell her the story of how I found the college. Amazingly, she was a great Christian and believed every word. I told her I'd like to come to look at the school and do a walk-through. She seemed elated that God had been so specific. She stated she'd talk to the president of the school, and she'd inform her of the situation. She did, and they called me back the next day.

Within a couple of weeks, I was making arrangements to go visit the college in Texas. I hadn't really told anyone else about it. I needed to have some time for it to all sink in. Over the next few weeks, I got the money for the flight, hotel, and car. It was at that time that I told Eric. He wasn't very happy about me leaving for a year, but I knew I had to. He was still clean and sober and doing well. He had almost a year clean. I had even been going to his AA meetings with him a couple of times a week. I thought to myself, *He'll be fine.* I flew out to visit the college that next month.

Bay Ridge College

I landed and picked up my rented car and headed to the college. The college was not technically in Houston like I thought. It was actually sixty miles south of Houston. As I was driving the van, I realized then that I was going farther and farther from the city. I especially recognized that it was more like a country. There were a lot of fields of cotton. It was something I had never seen (except on TV) and didn't know then at the time.

I found out later when I asked one of the school staff what were all the beautiful white flowers. It was then that they disclosed to me, laughingly, that they were not flowers but cotton. There were miles and miles of it. It made me reflect on my ancestors and how they were forced to pick it up during slavery. It was so low to the ground and full of thorns. It had to have been so hard on their backs, their hands and fingers, and then the thorns. It amazes me still how they skillfully picked it. They had to have gotten cut constantly by the thorns, yet they didn't bleed on the white cotton. It would have been obvious, and the cotton would be unsellable. That tells me that it took skills, like picking roses without getting stuck by thorns. It made me really have several emotions while driving.

When I finally reached the school and pulled into the parking lot, I couldn't believe it. The sign in front said "Bayridge Christian College," but it looked more like an elementary school in size. I asked myself "Is this a joke?" and sat back and started laughing. I spoke to God, "You have to be kidding me. You brought me all this way to this?"

Just as I was laughing, I heard God's voice say, "Sarah laughed." I remembered the story in the Bible of God telling Sarah, who was almost ninety at that time, that she would bear a child. I also remembered she'd laughed. God sent an angel to tell her good news. She had been unable to have children until then. So she laughed. She had a child nine months later at the age of ninety, and her husband, Abraham, was one hundred. The scripture plainly states that nothing is impossible with God.

I quickly wiped the smirk off my face and entered the building. The secretary was very kind. She had been the one who had taken my initial call. She was also the one to whom I told my story. We had a great conversation. She gave me a tour of the school. It was quite quaint actually. After the tour, I met the president of the school.

She was also an interim pastor. I met a few of the teachers. During the entire tour, I saw but one student. She was from Africa, and her name was Sarah. I just assumed the rest of the students were in their rooms or on break.

The president and her husband were kind enough to let me stay at their home. We had made prior arrangements. My room was almost seventy miles away. I understood now why they offered. DR and her husband were total opposites. She was a type A, very serious, and laughed seldom. He, on the other hand, was very relaxed and had a great sense of humor. Both were great hosts. They drove me to Houston and gave me a tour.

I attended the church where she was the interim pastor. She was a great preacher. I'd never really been around a female preacher. She was awesome. When my three days were up, I left confident that the school would be fine. The only thing that seemed to bother me was that they were the Church of God, which I knew nothing about.

I returned back to Seattle with a plan to attend the fall quarter, and I would move in the summer so I would be prepared for the first classes. I had a plan. Eric still wasn't happy about it. I knew it was something I had to do. I made an appointment with my pastor to inform him of my plans and to let him know I'd be leaving.

I was pleasantly surprised to find that the Church of God organization loved God, praised, and worshipped God just like me. I attended a Church of God annual Convocation in Atlanta that winter. I was so happy to find that out. Attending college would be fine. I was praying as I was bathing and preparing for one of the services in Atlanta. God dropped a jewel into me. He said, "Debby, you will be back in Atlanta, and you will do prison ministry." In a soft, quiet voice, God had given me another piece of my life. I wrote it down and hid it in my heart for future reference.

I returned to Seattle a happy camper. I now knew my purpose. I knew what I was to do next—go to school. It felt so good to know what I'd been searching for years—who I was and why I was made. I was going in circles looking for a purpose. Now I knew what I was to do.

CHAPTER 32

I started preparing for my move to Texas. One day in prayer, God made a statement to me. He said, "You must forgive your father." It kind of shook me because, over the last two years, I thought I had really worked on this. My father had another entire family. I knew all of my siblings. I had put my daughter in touch with him also. I really felt like the grudge I had held against him was gone. So I was truly surprised when God spoke those words to me.

Then he continued to say that talking to the hand was not forgiveness. This meant forgiving him but not dealing with him. Then he said, "You have to go and see him and talk to him." I was really stunned for a moment because I really believed I had forgiven him. I asked God to help me to do it. He was right. I said in my heart I'd forgiven him, but really, I hadn't because I wasn't dealing with him. I had great anxiety about doing it, but I prayed and asked God to give me the strength to do it.

When I arrived at his house, no one was there but him (which was unusual). Nervously, I said my hello, hugged him, and sat down. Now in my mind, I prepared this long speech I was going to give, but what came out was something totally different. I simply said, "Why did you leave me?" We both looked at each other, and for a moment, there was just an awkward quietness. Then he began to speak.

He began telling me of the troubles that he had with his wife who, back at that time, had the same struggles as him with alcohol. He said there were several times she left and went out in blackouts and was gone for weeks and months at a time. He stated how he would have to go find her. He told me of the arguing and fighting that went on. He said he was left to raise the kids himself a lot because of her drinking. The important thing he told me was that he had always checked on me through my uncle who was his friend. He said that at that time, he felt like I was doing well. I was in church as a kid going to school and really had small problems compared to what was going on at his house. He then said that he, at the time of my coming up, didn't believe he had any positive input to put into my life, so he just stayed away. He concluded with, "I'm very sorry," and that was it.

All my life I had thought that life was great for my sister and brothers. When I saw them all together, they in my mind looked so happy. I watched with envy as they were all on the beach together. I had always felt so excluded—only to find out that they were going through hell over here at their home.

My mom was a great mother and was always home with us, supporting me in all things I took part in. All of a sudden, I felt empathy for my dad and my siblings. I had always thought the grass was so much greener on the other side. As a child, I'd thought it was my fault he didn't come around. I thought I was unloved by him. I had wasted so many years assuming things that were not true. I never once took the time to talk to him. I had spent years looking for a father, feeling left out and unloved. I had it all wrong according to him.

At the moment, it felt like an elephant had been lifted off my chest. I was crying, and he was sad. He asked me to forgive him, and I did. My life changed, and my heart warmed to him. I realized that God had been right once again. We really both needed this conversation.

After we got through the tough part, we hugged. As I was sitting there, I noticed a picture on the fireplace mantle. It was strange because I'd been to the house on several occasions but had never remembered having seen it. It was an older picture of a woman. It got my attention because I looked somewhat like her. When I asked him who it was, he stated it was his mother. I said, "She looks young." That's when he told me that the picture was taken when she was forty.

As I picked the picture, I examined it closer, and we had several of the same features. I asked more questions and found out she was then eighty and was still living. She lived in Louisiana in his hometown still. I asked, "Did she know about me?" He said no. I told him I'd like to talk to her and if he thought that would be okay. He said yes. I got her number as I exited.

We hugged, and I left feeling elated. I called my mother and told her about my visit and how I'd gotten information about my newfound grandmother. I discussed with her about calling her. My mother had never met her or knew about her. My mom did say that it was common for Southern men to leave small towns and return but never inform their parents of their doings in the city. She was sure right about this. She was really happy about our meeting; it had been a long time coming.

I believe all three of us got freed from that one meeting. My dad and mom had both been young, and they dated, never married, and produced me. My dad married a year later, and they never really had contact after that. She did say he bought me one pair of walking shoes at nine months. Somehow, in one visit, we all got what we needed. Amazing!

Mom was actually excited about me calling my grandmother. The truth will make you free! I called my grandmother and told her who I was, and she just kept repeating, "I didn't know. I didn't know," as she cried on the phone. I had been a forty-year secret now let out of the box. I really truly believe that if I hadn't been obedient and gone over to talk to my dad like God asked me to, he would have gone to the grave and taken this secret with him, but it didn't happen.

As my grandmother and I talked, she asked about my mother. I told her some about her and that my mother encouraged me to make the call to her. I also told her of my move to Texas, which was not far from her, and asked if I could come to meet her with my mom once I'd gotten relocated. She was thrilled and said, "Yes, of course." I hung up the phone with my heart feeling so full. I'd always felt unloved and unwanted by that side of the family other than my aunt Ruby, only to find out within just a few days after all those years, I'd had it wrong.

I went to sleep that night so full and happy. I was going to meet my grandmother, and she wanted to meet me. I was so happy. I was really looking forward to moving now. I'd be within driving distance of my family.

As I was in the process of preparing to leave Seattle, Eric really was not happy with me leaving, but I knew I had to go. He had been clean and sober for over a year and was doing well. God had also told me in prayer to allow him to have one year with Eric for preparation for marriage. I'd agreed. It was something he and I had always agreed on since we'd met as young teens. We were going to get married. Unfortunately, neither of us went before God and asked him, but that's another part of the story. We were set on being husband and wife.

A couple of months later, I met with my pastor's wife (the pastor wasn't available) and told her of my endeavors and that I was heading toward Texas the next month. The pastor's wife prayed over me and gave me her blessings, and off I went down South.

My cousin Lena was great with cars, so she drove with me in the U-Haul down to Texas, and I bought her a one-way ticket back. The air-conditioning went out shortly after we left, so we had the windows open the entire trip. U-Haul did reimburse us though. My dorm was actually a full apartment, so all my furniture from my previous place fit in it perfectly. There was a couple who lived beneath us who rented the place but did not attend the school. They were seldom home except in the evenings. They both worked and had a small son.

I arrived in Texas in midsummer, and it was scorching hot. Most of the staff lived in housing right on campus or very nearby. Ironically, there was only one other student on campus at the time. Her name was Sarah, and she was from South Africa. We became friends quite quickly. Sarah was very bright, and she knew the scriptures well. Her English was near perfect. She had been taught both subjects well.

About a month after I got there, I asked my mom to fly in and drive with Sarah and I down to meet my father's mother who lived in Rodessa, Louisiana. My father agreed to meet us there also.

A dream came true for me, especially the little girl in me who had always longed to have my father and mother in the same room. I was so excited. I talked to my grandmother weekly since my move. For someone I'd never met, it seemed we'd known each other all along.

When we arrived at my grandmother's house, there was a warm welcome from the family to greet us. Some had driven from Augusta, Georgia, to come to meet me, and some were from Atlanta I'd known nothing about. Now my grandmother had been watching all the activity from her screened-in porch. I guess I must have taken too long to get to her because of the greetings from all the others. All of a sudden, it was like the parting of the Red Sea. Everyone moved to the side, and standing before me was this short beautiful older woman staring right up at me, leaning on her cane. Her hair was snow-white and braided back in one braid. She smiled and said, "There you are. I've been waiting since we talked on the phone to meet." Then she reached up and hugged me around the neck and just cried and kept saying, "I'm sorry. I just didn't know. I didn't know."

I cried, too, because I hadn't known about her either. As I looked around and saw all the family who had come to greet me, my heart was overwhelmed. I felt so complete. So full. So whole. Now I knew both sides of my family. I wasn't unwanted or unloved. I had just been unknown. That day and evening, my mom, Sarah, and I spent getting to know my cousins and extended family. We all cooked together and ate together. I went to sleep that night so thankful and grateful. I was loved. I thought, *They do love me.*

The next morning, my dad drove in. He had driven straight through the night twenty-four hours straight across the map as he stated. That morning, all my childhood dreams came true. I got to cook breakfast and sit down at the table with my mother, father, and grandmother as the others slept. I can't begin to describe the feelings I felt. There were so many emotions. I felt so blessed.

Later that morning, my aunt Ruby who had always looked out for me, and Uncle JT, my dad's brother, and several other family and friends came over and visited.

I had a large family. That afternoon, my grandmother, Sarah, my aunt Ruby, and I went for a drive in the country. Well, really it was all country. They just had one gas station, a restaurant, and one general store in Rodessa. My aunt took us to the family grave-yard and pointed out all the relatives who had passed on, one being my grandfather, my grandmother's husband. It was amazing to hear her name every person who was buried there. She had a photogenic memory. I was awed. We took lots of pictures, and my mother was taping my every movement since we'd arrived. At the time, I was slightly embarrassed, but I was so glad later when I got the chance to review the tapes.

As we were riding, my grandmother was pointing out the acres of land she owned. She told us she started in real estate. She said she'd planted quite a few watermelon seeds. That summer, she reaped quite a few—a truckload to be exact, she stated. Now by then, her husband had died, and she was left with five kids to raise. She said she was on her way to town to sell the individual watermelons when a man stopped her and inquired how much she would take for the entire truckload. She threw the number one hundred dollars out there, and he agreed. That was the start of her real estate.

She took that and bought a few mules so she could plant more watermelons. Then she bought more and more land. She, at that time, owned many acres of land and four or five houses that she rented out. She had become quite the businesswoman. She was known in the town as Ms. Jesse, "The Mayor of the Town." I was impressed and very proud.

As my grandmother grew weary of the ride, we dropped her back at the house, and we and my aunt continued our tour. I was amazed at her memory. She knew the background of every home and family, previous and present. It was she who pointed out the house of Sugar Ray, the fighter's home. I was surprised to learn that my grandma had been his sitter when he was young. She also noti-fied me of my kinship to Mike Tyson the fighter, who she said was a cousin. She was the best tour guide ever. She crossed every *T* and dotted all *I*s. She even showed us her family homes and the school she attended. She was an aunt by marriage. She'd been married to my father's brother for over thirty years at that time.

As I stated earlier, she was always so passionate about me, knowing my family ever since I could remember. She had always opened her house for me during my track and field days. She lived around the corner, and I rested there on several occasions. She was always regimented about having her kids speak to me and recognized that I was their cousin and Kenneth Wayne's daughter as they called him. I'd never told her, but she always made me feel part of the family and special. It wasn't until that day while we were riding through the country that I found some of the reasons why. She disclosed that she had also been the result of a second family. She explained to me that her father also had another whole family.

He had been married to his wife when he and her mother conceived her. She began to describe some of the challenges she had gone through as a child to be the side family—the whispers and talk and shame back then. She told me how she always felt left out on holidays and even on daily activities, sharing a married father. She was the secret that really wasn't a secret if you know what I mean. Her story was so similar to mine. Since Seattle was a lot larger, we didn't cross each other much other than our occasional running-ins at the public beach.

She told of how everyone knew in the small town of Rodessa. She and her mother weren't treated too kindly, to put it frankly. It was then that I finally understood why she took interest to include me in the family. I now knew why she opened her house and always made it known who my father was to all. She had never gotten that herself. She had been raised to be ashamed of her lineage without it being her fault.

I looked at my aunt Ruby with so much love. I'd always loved and appreciated the way she treated me. Now I felt so connected to her in such a different way. I was so glad she shared that story with me out of love. We kept driving until it got dark, and we arrived back at Grandma's.

Aunt Ruby and Uncle JT were staying at their own place they still owned in Rodessa. That evening, another wonderful thing happened. My aunt Ruby and Uncle JT invited my mom and dad over for fish dinner. Now imagine that. In twenty-four hours, my entire life had been changed. I met my long-lost grandmother and lots of my kin who I'd never known about or hadn't known about me either. I'd been able to cook and serve and enjoy breakfast with my mother, father, and grandmother. I'd gotten to know of my aunt Ruby's diligent love and share the same experience. That was an epiphany. Now my mother and father were having dinner together but not alone. Wow. I was truly overwhelmed with what God had done and was doing.

The next day, I learned a lot about the country and how they did things. Everything was sort of relaxed, and no one ever seemed to be in a hurry. It actually was a nice change. My cousins and I went down to the city mall, and I got a small tour of Shreveport, Louisiana—the Big City, they called it.

I had time to really sit and admire and get to know my grandmother. She told stories of her life while my mom was videotaping it all. She sat in her day dress with a great big pan, shucking peas. It was something I'd never seen or done before, but she accomplished it with ease. As she sat on the porch, several people drove through the self-made drive-through window in her home, which was nothing more than a carport. They would drive up, and she'd be sitting in her seat covered with a small blanket, which, I found out later, was there to conceal her licensed very large gun. When I asked her what she needed it for in the country, she stated for the rascals who were on drugs. To my surprise, the crack epidemic had even reached the country. She also handled lots of money.

She had, as I previously stated, three or four houses that she was renting out. I saw several different people bring her what she said was rent. I was intrigued by her sureness and quickness in mind even at eighty years old at the time. After watching her do business all day, I now realized why she was called the Mayor of the Town. She could be very kind but also be firm when needed. To the rascals who came by, her favorite saying to them was "to get in the middle of the road" (a phrase I use on the rascals I deal with now myself), and they would do just that—head off of her property down the walkway and into the middle of the road. I thought it was hilarious. At first, I thought she was a little hard, but as she told me more about the characters she called rascals, I soon understood.

Having had experience with drugs in the past, I knew how I had acted and what I'd do for more drugs. She was just protecting herself and being proactive by not listening to their many, many tall tales to get a few dollars for more drinks or drugs.

My mom, Sarah, and I really enjoyed our four-day stay. We all had to get back to Texas, and my cousins who traveled from Georgia needed to return home. We all embraced, cried some, and exchanged numbers and information. My friend Sarah got us all together in a large circle of about fifteen to twenty relatives and said a powerful, beautiful departing prayer. We three got in the rented car with my grandma standing on the porch waving her goodbyes. I waved back and promised to call, write, and see her soon. It was fantastic. I felt wonderful.

My dad was staying a few more days before he made the long drive across the country back to Washington State. He was in the yard waving also.

The drive back to the school was full of reminiscence of the family reunion. My mother and I were both happy, and Sarah was happy for us. My mother flew back to Seattle the following day.

CHAPTER 33

Sarah and I didn't have much, so we shared a lot of meals throughout the summer. Once, we were just sitting under the trees and found it was full of pecans. To both of our surprise, the entire college ground was full of them. We ate them as meals often.

I got a job cleaning the restrooms in the college that gave me a whole ninety dollars a month. Imagine I'd come from making over thirty dollars per hour nursing. That was definitely a humble pie for me. I did it with gladness. It was the only income I had coming in. During the summer, I got the opportunity to take a few trips along with the president of the school. One of those trips was to a beautiful college in Indiana. I thought about attending there. It was a much larger campus. We traveled there for a conference, and it was life changing. They offered different classes for the week. One of them, I remember, was going to jail, which allowed us an opportunity to go to the city jail and provide the jailers with a church service. This was accomplished only after a week of preparation in class.

Each of us signed up for a position such as singing, praying, or reading scripture. When everyone had signed up, the only position open was to be the minister and give a sermon to some one hundred men. I gave my first sermon that evening to about one hundred jailed men, and twenty or so gave their lives to Christ. It was amazing how God ordained that. Another one of the classes was an emotional abuse class. It dealt with those of us who suffered from all types of emotional abuse.

The teacher was a survivor herself and was very patient and kind to us all. She had several interactive activities that helped bring up some deep-rooted past hurts. It was the second time I'd had any counseling concerning childhood and young adult abuse. I felt the class really helped me share a lot of things I hadn't told anyone in years other than the psychologist I'd seen in Mount Vernon, Washington.

On the way back to the college, we (the president and her husband) stopped by one of the president's friends' home. It was the first time I'd been to a black person's house that had a pool. The house was gorgeous also, and I got a chance to ride in my first SUV (they were a new thing back then), and it was a Lincoln Navigator. I was truly impressed with DR. She had obtained so many degrees—two master's degrees and a PhD. She was an interim pastor. She'd come to Bay Ridge from the North. I don't think I had ever met anyone so schooled. She didn't know it, but I definitely admired her accomplishments.

The summer went by quickly. School started on time in September. There were only two active students on campus. Sarah and I both took the same classes. I found it odd that the college had been such a prestigious school. You could tell at one time it was top-notch for blacks. Something like a small More House School or Howard University. I never did find out the history of what happened to the school and why it emptied. On occasion, alma maters would stop in and share about their love for the school.

My schedule was full. I took four classes and chapel in between daily. The chapel consisted of the entire staff. We took turns leading it. It was good practice for what was to come for me.

There were ten of us in total in the school, including the maintenance guy.

The teachers were very efficient and educated in the Bible. It was basically like Sarah, and I had private schooling. I was glad Sarah was there. We made great study partners and schoolmates.

After school, we spent most of our evenings together as well. I sailed through the next two quarters. I was without much difficulty as a student.

One evening, I got a call no mother wants to receive. There were no cell phones back then, but we had a phone booth in the workout room on campus that I'd use to phone family, friends, and

Eric. This particular evening, Eric called and told me that someone took an assault gun and shot my daughter's godmother's beauty shop and that my daughter and one of her god sisters had been hit. I was hysterical. After I calmed down, Eric assured me that she was fine. He had been there to see her. She had just been braised in the head, but there was no damage done to her. Her god sister was shot in the leg, and a bullet had just missed the other sister. I was so thankful. I know God was with them all. I say that because when I did get a chance to talk to her godmother, she described the shooting. The first thing she said was, "There were angels with their hands up," fending off the bullet. She said the bullets would be coming straight but would ricochet off the hands of the guardian angels. She stated that the shooter had literally emptied his gun, and as small as the hair salon was, she felt like they all should have taken several bullets, but only one of her daughters had gotten hit. That bullet, she said, ricocheted from the arms of the angels. I believed her as she described the horrible encounter of him busting through the salon; he said nothing.

He had been an ex-boyfriend of one of the daughters. I was so thankful. At the time, I wanted to jump on the plane, but God told me to stay still and that everything would be fine. That was a hard thing to do at that time. You mean, I really had to trust him. It's easier to say than do, but I did. I stayed put. My daughter and her god sisters were fine, and I continued with my schooling.

Fall and winter quarters ended, and Christmas break came. I decided to go home for the holidays. I missed Eric and my family. I got a cheap ticket and headed to Seattle. I was so glad to be back home. It was nice and cool. I moved all my belongings to Texas, so I stayed at my sister's house. When I first got there, I was so excited to see Eric again. I'd been gone for almost nine months.

I called, but he never answered. He was missing in action. I didn't know because I had been gone, but he started using again. I was so hurt and confused. I called and talked to his mother. She'd seen him but didn't know then where he was. I spent the evening crying my eyes out. Where could he be, and why didn't he want to see me? The next day, I spent calling and looking around for him. I finally got him on the phone. He was still working at the dry cleaners, so I headed that way. He left early before I got there to avoid me. I just wanted to see him, but he'd told me he didn't want me to see him in the condition he was in—using. I didn't care. I should, though. I found him a few days later. We met up at his daughter's house, which was good because I got a chance to see her and the kids. She has five. We spent the evening together in her living room in each other's arms.

The next day, he went to work, and his daughter and I got a chance to spend some time and catch up.

It was then that she asked me a very particular question that threw me way off. I'd told her that his father told me he was using and had fallen off the wagon. That's when she asked me if he did tell me everything. I answered, "I thought that was it." That's when she began telling me about a lady named Kathy who her dad had been bringing over to her house and had been dating for a few months.

I told her, "I have no idea," but I knew who she was talking about exactly. I knew where she hung out—at the hall where I used to attend AA meetings with Eric, supporting his recovery. I was so angry with him. I called the hall immediately and asked for Kathy. Once she was on the phone, I told her who I was and that I was Eric's fiancée. She knew nothing about me either. He played us both. I hung up the phone, finished my visit with his daughter, and waited for him to get off of work. I was going to act like everything was okay when I picked him up, and once I had him in the car, I was going to drop the bombshell that I knew of his little rendezvous with Kathy. That's exactly what I did.

Of course, he said he was sorry and gave me the I-missed-you spiel. "I was lonely. You were so far away," he went on to say. I just listened. Lies! Lies! Lies! I wanted to believe him so badly. I did, but I wasn't going to take a chance with my body though. It had been nearly nine months since I'd been gone and since I'd had sex with him up until the previous night. My gut told me to get myself checked out. The next day, he, his daughter (for support), and I went to the hospital to get checked out. It was known that Kathy slept around a lot and possibly had hepatitis C, I'd heard. Eric and I both got our results back, and they both were positive for hepatitis C. I really wanted to choke him, but I just dropped him off at his mother's house, dropped his daughter off at home, and headed back to my sister to collect myself. Hepatitis C—there was no cure. It really took me a few days to collect myself. I thought I was so in love. We'd always vowed our love for each other. It seemed it was and always had been one-sided.

Over the next week, he assured me that it wasn't true. He spoke of his enduring love for me over the past twenty years (we met when he was nineteen and I was fifteen) and how he still wanted to marry me and continued where we had left off before I left. I took it all in because I wanted to agree to still marry him. He vowed to clean himself back and get back on the wagon. We set a date for January 23. I was supposed to start back to school that week. I told myself that it would be okay and that I'd only be two weeks late.

Eric and I agreed to tie the knot, and I'd head back to finish out the college year. It didn't happen that way. We got married and had a beautiful wedding. Everyone seemed to have been waiting for us to jump the broom after over twenty years. Everyone pitched in. My cousin who was a fabulous event decorator did the event for free. My aunt bought the rings. My cousin bought my dress, and my sister bought my reception dress. The Esquire Club, where we had our family reunions just the week before, charged us just a few dollars, and someone paid for that. Family and friends cooked food. Both my father and my stepfather walked me down the aisle. My niece, while I was waiting in the dressing room to walk out, was constantly asking me if I was sure and that I could change my mind at any time. It was a whirlwind wedding—all accomplished in ten days. Eric's niece had gotten us a suite in a downtown hotel, and the room was decorated to match the wedding. I was so happy, and so was he.

We moved in with his mom the next day. All seemed well until I called the school to let them know of my whirlwind marriage and that I'd be returning over the next few days. To my surprise, they said that I could not come back and that the quarter was in two weeks. They wished me well and told me that I needed to come and move my things. I was devasted. I thought that since they only had two students, one being me, they would bend the rules a bit. They didn't. I'd have to move back to Seattle.

At first, I got very upset about the school's decision. When I came to grips with it, I decided to let go, move on, and start a new life with my now-husband, Eric Barnett.

Together, Eric and I took the journey down South to retrieve my apartment full of furniture from the campus. Because we did not have a honeymoon, we went straight to mom's. We made the trip our honeymoon. I luckily found an inexpensive apartment through the Little Nickel Want Ads after two weeks. We asked for financial gifts at the wedding. The money covered the move-in costs. Thank God. I really didn't want to continue living with mom.

I felt like since we were married, we needed our own place. Even though Mom was gracious enough to let us stay as long as we needed, I was excited about the trip. We stopped first in Las Vegas. We had a nice time for a few days there. I never was a gambler, but I enjoyed just being with my husband. We took a week to get to the campus, stopping frequently to take in the scenery and to act like newlyweds.

Once we got there, it didn't take us long to pack up the U-Haul we'd reserved. I said my goodbyes to all staff and Sarah, and we were headed back to Washington with our belongings in tow behind us. We snuggled in the large truck back up to Seattle. We made the trip in two days back.

Once we got to the apartment, I unpacked quickly and got our home livable with joy. Eric still had his managerial position at the dry cleaners. I, of course, hadn't worked in almost a year. I saw him off to work every morning, gladly packed a lunch, and sent him out the door with a kiss. That worked for about three months, and all of a sudden, it hit me that I'd given up school. It rained continuously for the first month I was back, which was so difficult from the sunny days I'd had in Texas. I really became clinically depressed for the first time in my life. On top of that, I needed a hysterectomy because I had several fibroids. That was done, and that threw me into an estrogen depletion on top of my depression. Eric started disappearing days at a time. He was using again.

I got a job at a nursing facility in West Seattle but was out for surgery for six weeks. I'd never been so deeply depressed before, so I really had no way of dealing with it. I just cried a lot and slept a lot. Eric was barely coming home but to change clothes and eat every now and then, and I was stuck with myself. I finally got counseling that winter and had six weeks of sessions with a great therapist. At the end of the sessions, I asked for more, but the therapist felt like I had enough. He stated that I was all right and doing very well by his standards compared to what I had put myself through for years. He thought that I should make some decisions about whether to stay in my dysfunctional marriage. He also pointed out that one of my largest, toughest problems was that I picked men like my father—men, he stated, who were unavailable. His statement hit me like a brick.

I can remember getting in the car and trying to drive, and I couldn't because I was crying so hard. Was it true? I sat on the side of the road bawling my eyes out.

I came to the realization that he was right. As I sat there reflecting on past relationships, they all were with people who somehow were unavailable to love me like I deserved. It seemed odd because I had never been around my dad much, but that fit the diagnosis. He had been unavailable. When I really got honest, all my past and present relationships were just that—unavailable.

I actually cried for over two hours in the car. It was actually a good thing because now I knew the problem. I just needed a solution. The week before, I cut all my hair off. I knew through this revelation that it was not my hair that needed cutting but my heart that needed fixing. By this time, my husband was having a relationship with the choir director in the new church he had brought me to. I never went back to mine. I was trying to follow his lead. He didn't know how. He cheated, drugged, and drank his way through the next months. I was so hurt and devasted, but somehow, I got through it.

CHAPTER 34

One day, I prayed and asked God, *Why am I having to go through all the challenges with him?* That's when he very clearly and sternly, with love, told me that I had brought the trouble on myself. He told me that he'd asked me to let him have Eric for a year and to go to school in Texas. He reminded me that I made the choice to leave school and try to fix things on my own by marrying Eric in nine months, not a year. I was supposed to be in Texas, not in Seattle. The suffering I had was self-made. I had blatantly disobeyed him. This was my consequence. I'd have to deal with it.

I cried out to the Lord and said I was sorry, but nothing really changed as far as my situation, but my heart changed. At least God was talking to me again. I poured myself into the twelve-step program I found when I was supporting Eric the previous year. I prayed a lot and waited to be released from the predicament I'd placed myself in—marriage.

I also got involved in some of the outreach programs at church. I worked on the board of the recovery programs. I don't know how, but I managed to keep my sanity. My daughter had my second grandchild in June 2000. That was a real delight and kept me going for a while. It was in August though when I had a little glimmer of hope. My eldest niece was moving to Atlanta. Out of nowhere, she decided to move. She said she was concerned about her two young sons becoming involved in gangs, and they were very young. They had a lot of gang influence around Seattle at that time. A lot of gang members from Los Angeles fluctuated in the Seattle area. She asked if Eric and I could fly the kids down. She had three. She was going to drive a U-Haul and didn't want them to have to make the long hot trip down. Eric somehow was around and agreed to fly with me and the kids to Atlanta, Georgia.

It was so hot. The last time I'd been there was in January, and there had actually been a small bit of snow on the ground during the Church of God conference. It was sweltering, but it felt so good to leave Seattle and get away from what was a failing marriage. We dropped the kids off. With my niece, Eric and I both vowed we'd be back. We both loved the culture and the heat. When we returned home, Eric went right back to his tactics, missing days and nights. It was soon after we got back that God himself released me to go to Atlanta. I actually started packing a box a day, and he never realized that they were stacking around the wall in the living room. Every time he would show back up, I'd remind him of our decision to move to Atlanta, and I'd advise him that I was still going to make the move. He stayed so loaded. I don't believe he even heard me most of the time.

The fall came, and Eric was still using and gone most nights. I was usually crying myself to sleep. I really thought I could fix him. It wasn't until then that I realized it wasn't my job. It was God's. I hadn't given God the time he asked me to give him with Eric. I spent many days and nights wondering how different it would have been if I would have been obedient and stayed in Texas and given Eric the year with God. I'll never know. I just knew I had to work on myself. That's the only somebody I could fix. That comes out of the twelve-step program. In the serenity prayer, it states,

> God, grant me the Serenity to accept the things I cannot change [others]
> The courage to change the things I can [me]
> and the wisdom to know the difference.

I really truly learned a lot from the twelve-step program I attended frequently and especially from that prayer.

November came, and my cousin Lena and I, along with a few of the fellows in the twelve-step fellowship, packed up the entire apartment (Eric had moved back in with his mother) into a moving van and were heading off to Atlanta. I'd promised her if she drove down with me, I'd fly her back home. She agreed. As we were filling up the van with gas, Eric called. He must have gone by the apartment and seen it was vacant, or someone may have informed him. Anyway, he asked where we were, and I told him. Somehow, in my heart, I think all along I was hoping that he would come. I thought possibly that a new place would give us a possible new start.

It didn't happen that way. He drove up and just looked shocked. He was shocked to see us. It was as if he really didn't believe I was leaving. He just stood there looking at us drive off. Never did he say, "I want to go with you." My heart was broken, but I kept moving. My cousin Lena and I took the ocean view Highway 101 so we could see the ocean. It added a day to our travels, but we cut across the states and arrived in Atlanta without any problems. By this time, my niece had gotten her own house. I had a few family members, about five, who helped me get my stuff into storage temporarily. I exhaled for the first time in a long time.

Being in Atlanta was like a breath of fresh air. Seeing new places and new faces seemed to wipe the deep depression right away. The fact that the sun shines just about every day helped also. My niece and I got along well, along with her three children. My cousin lived down in Atlanta, and he checked on us frequently. I didn't go to work right away. I really needed restoration after the storm I'd been through in Seattle.

My niece worked, and I stayed home with the children when they were not in school. I talked to Eric occasionally, but nothing had changed with him until one evening when he called and said God had spoken to him and told him to come to Georgia with me. At first, I was very skeptical, but he'd never used that line before, so I believed him.

He came down, and all went well for a while until he found a crack house down in Georgia. They say you can find what you're looking for anywhere. He left and went back to his mother's house, where he always ran to. I was devastated and had to pick myself up once again and pull myself together. I did, but it took a while.

I found a job in Marietta, a dialysis clinic. The drive was quite far, but they paid me what I'd asked for. Within a year, I'd moved into my own apartment. I started dating a younger guy, but that didn't work out, and a year later, I bought my home where I reside now.

Approximately three years later, I met Michael, and we became friends fairly quickly.

I began doing missions, and I also did some jail ministries (that was a prophecy fulfilled). One of my mission trips was to Haiti. The trip was very successful. A Haitian pastor and I, along with four other missionaries, did a two-week Bible vacation school. We had over two hundred kids each day.

When I returned, I was diagnosed with stage 4 breast cancer. By the time I gave my report to the church, God healed me completely, and I was able to share the healing with the entire church.

God is great! During the course of my breast cancer scare, I came very close to the LORD. He is a faithful God and a true healer. Going through it also brought Michael and I closer. He was there through the entire process with me.

For the next three years, we grew closer. We attended church together and became engaged in 2006. On January 31, 2007, we were married.

I was doing prison and jailhouse ministry for the next year. It was challenging but rewarding. I also attended Bible university in Decatur, Georgia.

In 2007, Michael was diagnosed with chronic kidney failure. It was a big blow to him and me, especially being that I'd been working in dialysis for years.

At first, things went well. Together, we did ministries and began housing people from all walks of life in our home. We would get them jobs and get them set up to get back in the mainstream of things.

I had been housing people on my own since I had my apartment and continued once I bought the house, but it was good to have Michael along with me doing ministry for God. We'd housed over one hundred people by 2011.

In 2012, we opened a church in the living room of our house. I'd been ordained in 2008 at the church we were attending and installed our own church in 2012. God was doing some marvelous things with the church. Many lives were changed. Though the church was small, the Holy Spirit brought much power. All was well until Michael suddenly passed in 2013 on Easter Sunday. It truly was a shock for me and one of the most difficult days of my life. My Michael was gone. Losing my best friend was one of the hardest things I'd ever done in my life.

I never returned back to work after Michael's death. Instead, I took two eleven-week grief counseling courses, which were a blessing and exactly what I needed.

While I was taking the first eleven-week course, my mother was attending the course with me. Then she had a bleeding stroke, was hospitalized, and had to have emergency brain surgery. It was another awful scare. The thought of losing another best friend (which my mom is to me) was really more than I could have taken. I fell to my knees and told God so in the small chapel of the hospital. He spared her life. I believe it would have been too much, and his word says he will not put more on you than you can bear (1 Corinthians 10:13).

I really believe in my heart of hearts that it would have been too much.

My mom came through the surgery with flying colors. She was healthy and remains healthy still at eighty-nine, living on her own. To God be the glory!

Once we got through my mother's rehab, I was able to continue my grief counseling. It was Christian based, and I recommend it highly.

After the loss of Michael, I continued with the ministry and the church. I continued to house people, and I added an outreach feeding program where we feed the people on the streets of Atlanta every week.

Five years later, in 2017, I met and married John Young. I met him through his daughter on one of our outreach feeding ministries. We met in April and were married nine months later in February of 2018. John is and has always been supportive of the ministry.

After losing Michael, I really thought that marriage was not in my future. I just stayed close to God and stayed faithful to the ministry, and God sent me a king.

We continue to carry the gospel of Jesus Christ in as many ways as we can. I do this because I know the loving God I serve and what he's done for me. He brought me from the low places—the street prostitution and drugs—and has set me at the table with kings and queens. He changed me from the inside out. If he did it for me, he can and will do it for anyone (John 3:16).

I truly serve a loving God of second chances. I do and will continue to share the good news of Jesus Christ with all I come across who want to have a better life. To date, we have housed over two hundred lost souls through our housing and ministry.

I am so thankful for my Lord and Savior Jesus Christ who kept me through a life of horror. He took my ashes and gave me beauty (Isaiah 61:3).

He is and always will be first in my life. I know he is the only one and true God (Isaiah 45:5–12).

And that is and always will be the true black and white of it.

> I waited patiently for the Lord: and he inclined unto me, and he heard my cry. He brought me up also out of a horrible pit, out of the miry clay, and set my feet upon a rock and established my goings. And he hath put a new song in my mouth, even praise unto our God; many shall see it, and fear, and shall trust in the Lord. Blessed is that man that make the the Lord his trust, and respecteth not the proud, nor such as turn aside to lies. Many O Lord my God are thy wonderful works which thou hast done, and thy thoughts which are to us-ward: if I would declare and speak of them, they are more than can be numbered. Amen. (Psalm 40:1–5)

ABOUT THE AUTHOR

Debby Young is a wife, mother of one beautiful daughter, and grandmother to three wonderful grandchildren. Debby is also blessed to still have both her mother and father ages eighty-eight and eighty-nine, respectively. Debby was born and raised in the beautiful northwest of Seattle, Washington. Debby came from a large family of nine. She has five sisters and two brothers. She was raised in the Lake Washington area. Debby moved to Atlanta, Georgia, in 2000. She was ordained in the year 2009. In 2012, Restoration for Life Ministries Inc.'s door was opened. Debby is a senior pastor. Housing for Life bloomed from the church also, which has housed over two hundred people from all walks of life. Food for Life was started and is another branch. It is an outreach food ministry that has also fed hundreds of homeless people over the last ten years. Debby is a woman who cherishes her relationship with her Lord and Savior Jesus Christ. Her goal is to show as many people as she can the true love of Jesus Christ.